SCARLET TUNIC

**The badge of the Royal Canadian
Mounted Police with its motto
"Maintain the Right."**

Robert Gordo

FRONT COVER

The empty Red Tunic of the RCMP is symbolic of the loneliness of the Police Officer. The frog's role is explained in the book, the decorations with it are the RCMP Long Service Medal and the Canadian Cross of Valour, both treasured along with the memory of Clarence and Police Service Dogs Smokey and Talon. The undress ribbons on the tunic are (left to right) Cross of Valour, Long Service Medal, and the Commissioner's Commendation for Bravery. The revolver is RCMP issue, Smith & Wesson Model 10, .38 Special.

Copyright © 1994 Robert Gordon Teather

Canadian Cataloguing in Publication Data

Teather, Robert Gordon, 1947-
    Scarlet tunic

ISBN 1-895811-52-X

1. Police patrol — British Columbia — Surrey. 2. Royal Canadian Mounted Police.
I. Title
HV7914.T42 1997   363.2'32'0971133   C97-910958-2

First Edition - 1994   Second Edition - 1997

HERITAGE HOUSE PUBLISHING COMPANY LTD.
UNIT #8, 17921 55TH AVE., SURREY, B.C.

Printed in Canada

CONTENTS

WARNING!

The techniques explained in this book are to be used only by people who have been trained in their use. The "Police Sleeper Hold," more commonly referred to as "Carotid Control," will induce unconsciousness without pain or discomfort in 10 to 15 seconds. It must be practiced only under adequate supervision by a trained instructor. The "Rewkaido" technique used to stop the heart and paralyze the diaphragm is as real as the "Vulcan Nerve Pinch" popularized by Star Trek's Mr. Spock. It must not be attempted except under supervision by a trained instructor.

ACKNOWLEDGMENTS

Scarlet Tunic is a true story about friendship, strength and under-standing. It is also a story of survival. Throughout my life, I have met a few incredibly strong and wonderful people who have extended their hand of friendship when I needed it most.

TO

Chief Bill Heckler (and friends) who showed they cared and encouraged me when I was about to quit.

My dear friend Brian Powell — a brave and honest friend who now lives in a greater world.

Constable Shirley Hall. A fighter extraordinaire and a true friend.

Leonard Krygsveld, who entered my life during my loneliest hours and offered compassion and friendship.

Art Downs, my publisher and friend. Thanks, Art, for your en-couragement, support and late night calls to remind me that punctua-tion is important

Corporal Bill Henderson and Police Service Dog Talon, who saved my life by protecting me after I had been beaten unconscious by a gang of youths.

Sergeant Tom Haworth and Police Service Dog Smokey, two dear friends with whom I have shared long nights and laughter.

AND

To my beautiful wife, Susan, who has always stood behind me, encouraged me and loved me through my toughest years. I love you, Susan.

THE AUTHOR

Corporal Robert "Bob" Gordon Teather is a veteran with 27 years of service in the RCMP. During his career he has won the highest award in the RCMP, the Commissioner's Commendation for Bravery, and Canada's highest award, the Canadian Cross of Valour. The latter decoration was awarded for rescuing two fishermen trapped in an air pocket of an overturned boat two miles off the B.C. Coast. Bob was only the thirteenth Canadian to win the Cross of Valour.

His past duties have included Uniform Patrol where he was nearly killed by teenage thugs who clubbed him from behind. For seven years he was a Hostage Taker-Barricaded Person Negotiator and negotiated the surrender of many armed and barricaded people. As a Diving Instructor he trained and equipped a team of Police Officers to provide all public safety diving for the Province of B.C. He was personally involved in over 200 operational cases, most of which involved recovering the bodies of people who drowned.

He has lectured to police officers, firefighters, doctors and many citizens and others throughout Canada and the U.S. on diving techniques, underwater crime scene photography, ice diving procedures, underwater wireless voice communication and similar topics. In addition, he has helped produce several cassettes. One of them is a 2 1/2-hour program on techniques for notifying and aiding next of kin of people involved in a diving tragedy.

Scarlet Tunic is his fourth book. The others are *Merlin*, a novel about a public safety diver, *The Underwater Investigator* and *Encyclopedia of Underwater Investigation*. As the name suggests, the *Encyclopedia* is a complete guide to underwater investigation and is being sold all over the world.

Since graduating from the RCMP's Training Academy in Regina in 1968, Bob has compiled a distinguished service record. One of the men to whom he dedicated this book, Corporal Don Withers, would be very proud of his accomplishments.

DEDICATION

TO ALL CENTURIONS —
PAST, PRESENT AND FUTURE
WHO WOULD SACRIFICE
EVERYTHING

AND

TO JAKE, E.T. AND
CORPORAL DON WITHERS
ADIOS, FRIENDS

A HERITAGE IS BORN

The Royal Canadian Mounted Police has a heritage dating back to 1873 with the formation of the North-West Mounted Police. Contrary to popular belief, the role of these new policemen wasn't to protect white settlers against Indians. It was to protect Indians from the whites. In this case the whites were U.S. whiskey peddlars who controlled what is today Southern Alberta. From a series of trading posts they were destroying the Indians with booze and bullets.

Biggest of these posts was Fort Whoop-Up near present-day Lethbridge — today rebuilt as an historical attraction. Completed in 1872, it took 30 men two years to build and included a heavy timbered palisade with loopholes for rifles, corner bastions with cannon and its own flag. Indians pushed their buffalo hides and other items through a small wicket for home-made "whiskey" in a tin cup. When their furs were gone they traded their horses and even their wives and daughters as young as 12.

Probably the most damning indictment against the whiskey traders was written by the Reverend John McDougall, one of the West's renowned missionaires. He noted: "Scores of thousands of buffalo robes and hundreds of thousands of wolf and fox skins and most of the best horses the Indians had were taken south into Montana, and the chief article of barter for these was alcohol. In this traffic very many Indians were killed, and also quite a number of white men. Within a few miles of us ... forty-two able-bodied men were the victims among themselves, all slain in the drunken rows. These were Blackfoot .... There was no law but might. Some terrible scenes occured when whole camps went on the spree, as was frequently the case, shooting, stabbing, killing, freezing, dying.

"Thus these atrocious debauches were continuing all that winter not far from us. Mothers lost their children. These were either frozen to death or devoured by the myriad dogs of the camp. The birth-rate decreased and the poor red man was in a fair way towards extinction."

Stamping out this whiskey traffic in a lawless land which extended 800 miles from Manitoba to the Rockies was the duty of the new North-West Mounted Police. By October the first 150 recruits — only two with police experience — arrived at Lower Fort Garry near present-day Winnipeg. They had survived their first test — a brutal 450-mile canoe and portage trip through the wilderness. But much worse was to come.

Training began immediately, with 12 hours a day spent in foot drill, marksmanship, riding and other duties. In charge of teaching horsemanship was Sergeant-Major Samuel B. Steele, destined to

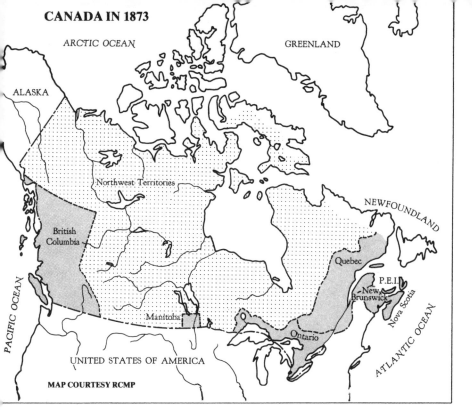

CANADA IN 1873

ARCTIC OCEAN

GREENLAND

ALASKA

Northwest Territories

NEWFOUNDLAND

British
Columbia

PACIFIC OCEAN

Quebec

P.E.I.
New
Brunswick

Nova Scotia

ATLANTIC OCEAN

Manitoba

Ontario

UNITED STATES OF AMERICA

MAP COURTESY RCMP

Canada in 1873.

Taken in 1874, the photo below is probably the earliest one of the NWMP.
Seated is Sub-Inspector John French, later killed during the Riel Rebellion.
Standing behind him is Sub-Inspector F. J. Dickens, son of author Charles
Dickens, who had to abandon Fort Pitt during the Rebellion.

become the most famous of all the Mounties. Of the training, he noted: "...if the temperatures were not lower than 36 below zero the riding and breaking should go on.... With plenty of such exercise, when spring opened they were very fine riders...."

On July 8, under 32-year-old Commissioner George A. French, the Force left Dufferin in Manitoba on their 800-mile wilderness trek. Included were 275 policemen, 339 horses, 142 oxen, 114 Red River carts, 73 wagons and two cannon which weighed a ton each and would wear out horses and men who had to help pull them. Because there were no settlers along the route, the Force had to be self-sufficient, with mowing machines, rakes and other farm implements part of their equipment. They would have to shoe their horses, grow feed and vegetables, build barracks, doctor themselves and their animals and live entirely cut off from assistance. Youngest member of the force was 16-year-old Fred Bagley. He was to serve 25 years and Old Buck, the horse he rode, lived to be over 30.

The men's uniform was a scarlet Norfolk jacket, gray breeches and blue trousers with a double white stripe. For headgear they had a white pith helmet and a pill-box hat, totally useless for protection against sun, wind and all other elements.

The inappropriate headgear was only the first indignity inflicted on the men. Their rifles were obsolete single shot. By contrast, the Indians and whiskey traders had Winchesters and other repeaters. Their British revolvers were also inferior to those in the West, and their tents were to be summarized as "...a fraud on the prairie."

Another obstacle was the lack of information. The prairie was still the home of the Indians, with herds of buffalo stretching over the horizon. The only map they had was dated 1861 and proved unreliable, as did their guides. When the policemen finally found Fort Whoop-Up, it was 80 miles from where they had believed it was.

But their biggest foe, not only during the trek but also in forth-coming years, was Ottawa politicians and bureaucrats.

Commissioner French wanted to follow the U.S.-Canada border where Boundary Commission surveyors had built a trail in 1872-74. But he was ordered to leave the trail after 200 miles, head northward then west. Because the politicians who gave the order knew nothing about the region, the men were condemned to unnecessary hardship and many horses and oxen to death. For weeks they travelled through a parched land with infrequent waterholes, no wood for fires and animals competing with grasshoppers, buffalo and prairie fires for food.

"Camped beside a marsh pool which had dried up. Got a few buckets of water by digging in mud ... no wood or water," was a frequent entry in Commissioner French's diary. Summer heat was another torment, with the cavalcade usually travelling by 4 a.m. The heat, lack of feed and water, the heavy cannon and two mortors, and literally clouds of mosquitoes quickly incapacitated the horses.

After only 10 days French wrote "...two horses left on road, being unfit to travel." His diary for July 22 notes: "No wood or water during morning march or afternoon march.... I insisted on men dismounting and walking on foot every alternate hour and propose continuing this to relieve the horses."

On July 25 they had covered only 300 miles of the estimated 800. By now it was increasingly obvious that many — if not all — of the animals would die. As a result, French disobeyed his original orders to keep the Force together. To avoid disaster, he split into three groups — one returning to Fort Ellice, one going northwestward to Fort Edmonton, the other continuing towards the Rockies. The Fort Edmonton group under Inspector Jervis and Sergeant-Major Sam Steele were three months fighting their way to the Hudson's Bay Company's trading post. Of the trip, Inspector Jervis noted of the horses: "They were living skeletons."

Men and animals in the main group shared the suffering. On September 3 French noted: "There being no grass, had to make ... 17½ miles without halting. Next stage 20 miles, no water."

Sub-Constable E.H. Maunsell wrote: "Although it was fortunate that we had buffalo meat to eat, being out of provisions, still straight boiled meat soon palled on the palate. We were all attacked with diarrhea, which greatly weakened us. Not only did we eat boiled buffalo meat, using their dried dung for fuel, but on occasions were forced to drink diluted buffalo urine.... Our poor horses suffered greatly, both from lack of food and water...."

On September 12 the greatly weakened Force reached the junction of the Belly and Bow Rivers, the supposed location of Fort Whoop-Up. There was no Fort. It was, in fact, some 80 miles away. But now the Mounties ill-fortune changed. Commissioner French and some of his men headed 100 miles southward to the U.S. outpost of Fort Benton on the Upper Missouri River.

Here they met Isaac Baker who had financed construction of Fort Whoop-Up for his nephew, Alfred Hamilton. Isaac — and other Fort Benton merchants — were friendly and helpful. Isaac introduced French to a half-breed guide called Jerry Potts who was promptly hired at $90 a month. Potts proved remarkable, his sense of direction — even in a blizzard — was amazing to the policemen. He was to serve the force for 22 years and when he died Sam Steele noted: "As scout and guide I have never met his equal, he had none in the North West or the States to the south."

Under Potts the Mounties finally reached Fort Whoop-Up on

October 9. Commissioner Macleod and Potts rode up to the gate. But instead of the "hot work" which French had expected, they found that, as Potts had predicted, the whiskey peddlars had fled. Only bearded Dave Akers remained. He invited the pair to "Come right in."

Macleod offered to buy the outpost for $10,000, but Akers wanted $25,000. When Macleod decided to build their own post, Potts led them 60 miles to an island in the Oldman River. Here the policemen started work on the first NWMP post in the Canadian West, named Fort Macleod after Colonel Macleod.

Even while the policemen were living in tents and building the post, others were out on patrol. A few days after their arrival Colonel Macleod noted that they "...struck a first blow at the liquor traffic in this country."

A patrol arrested five men who were promptly fined. One of them was later shot and killed while trying to escape. Later the Mounties learned that he was wanted in Eastern Canada for murder and also had killed a Blackfoot Indian. By spring the whiskey traffic had largely disappeared, those involved quickly learning that "...the Mounted Police didn't scare worth a cent."

The Indians soon realized that the Mounties were their friends. In 1877 when the Blackfoot Nation gathered to sign a treaty, Crowfoot, their legendary Chief, stated: "If the Police had not come to the country where would we all be now? Bad men and whiskey were killing us so fast that very, very few of us would have been left today. The Police have protected us as the feathers of a bird protect it from winter...."

To help police the plains, two additional forts were built. One was Fort Walsh to the southeast near the U.S. border. It was later abandoned but today has been restored and is a feature attraction in Cypress Hills Provincial Park which straddles the Alberta-Saskatchewan border. The other fort was named Calgary and around it grew Alberta's second largest city.

Controlling the whiskey traffic resulted in three deaths. In October 1874, Constable Godfrey Parks died of typhoid, and in December Constables Baxter and Wilson were caught in a blizzard and froze to death.

The next challenge for the Mounties began in 1876 when the warlike Sioux retreated into Canada after slaughtering Lieutenant-Colonel George A. Custer and his entire 7th Cavalry. Eventually there were some 6,000 Sioux in the Cypress Hills under Chief Sitting Bull, with only a few red coats under Superintendent J.M. Walsh to control them. Despite massive problems they succeeded and by 1881 all of the Indians had returned to the U.S.

Four years later the Riel Rebellion erupted and many policemen served with distinction. In the forefront was Sam Steele who commanded a group of settlers, cowboys and policemen called Steele's Scouts. They were part of a force which pursued Chief Big Bear whose braves had massacred eight white men, including two priests. Women and children were taken captive and spent 70 days on the trail with the fleeing Indians, daily expecting to be killed. After a series of battles in which a number of Indians and Steele's Scouts were wounded or killed, the prisoners were released.

For their tenacity and bravery, Steele's Scouts received not thanks from Ottawa beaurocrats and politicians but shabby treatment. While soldiers who served received a medal within a year, the policemen had to wait three years before their contribution was grudgingly acknowledged. Astonishingly, the citizen members of Steels's Scouts were denied a medal because they "...hadn't been in action," even though they were the first to be shot at and some had been wounded or killed.

For the Mounties, the campaign ribbon was only one example of ungrateful treatment by Ottawa. In 1879, the policemen's pay was virtually halved, with a sub-Constable's reduced from 75 cents a day to 40 cents — and not returning to 75 cents for over 25 years. As a further insult, the free grant of 160 acres at the end of a satisfactory enlistment was cancelled. In 1883 at Fort Macleod the men staged a revolt to protest the conditions. For months they had been fed bread, beef and tea three times a day, the meat frequently fit only for garbage. Uniforms were not replaced and on their cut-rate wages the men had to borrow money and pay interest to feed and clothe themselves. Among clothing all men bought were Stetson cowboy hats since the pill-box type was useless for Western weather. The pill-boxes weren't officially replaced until 1897, nearly a quarter century after they were first issued.

In 1874 Commissioner French refused to use a new post at Swan River because he felt that the barracks were unfit to live in. Two years later he resigned because of a continuing clash with politicians.

The Force's fourth Commissioner, L.V. Herchmer, was also appalled at conditions and worked to improve them. One change was replacing the tents that were "a fraud on the prairie." Among their faults was that the shape didn't permit the use of bunks. The men had to sleep on the ground, with rheumatism often the consequence. Proper sleeping facilities were denied the men even in the barracks. As Herchmer indignantly noted: "The Indians at the Industrial School have beds. Yet the police, the finest body of men in the country, still sleep on boards and trestles."

It was a credit to the Mounties that despite the shabby treatment, they faithfully upheld the Force's motto "Maintain the Right." In the 1890s, for instance, thousands of settlers arrived in the West. (An Indian summarized the influx as "The plains were black with white men.") Since most of the settlers had no experience of hazards such as blizzards, prairie fires, and isolation, the Mounties listed every settler and began a regular patrol. The distance they travelled was awesome. In one year out of Regina alone patrols travelled 350,000 miles, an average of almost 1,000 miles a day — on horseback or in a buggy.

In 1895 the Yukon was added to their duties. Then three years later the Klondike gold rush erupted and hordes of men stampeded north. Sam Steele, now a Superintendent, was placed in command. Since there was no food in the Yukon, Steele ordered that every man had to bring in a ton of supplies. With only 285 men, Steele controlled some 50,000 stampeders and, in the spring of 1898, checked over 7,000 boats as the gold-hungry men embarked on a perilous trip down the Yukon River to Dawson City.

In 1904, the policemen's 30 years of service was recognized by King Edward VII. He decreed that henceforth the Force would be called the Royal North-West Mounted Police. Then in 1920 came another name change to today's familiar Royal Canadian Mounted Police.

But as the following pages will reveal, the heritage inherited from the Mounties of 1873 still flourishes.

Art Downs
Surrey, B.C.

AUTHOR'S FOREWORD

The Royal Canadian Mounted Police is known worldwide. Every post-card and souvenir shop in Canada carries the image of the well-known Scarlet Tunic and, if you were to ask anyone who the "Mounties" are, you will hear mention of history, tradition, bravery and honor. Mostly, however, the image is that of the famed Scarlet Tunic which forms a part of their dress uniform.

Few people know what goes on inside the uniform and inside the hearts of our "Mounties" after they are sworn-in and are charged with the responsibility of upholding the laws of Canada. In an attempt to fill this information void many books have been written on the history of the RCMP and that is good. In addition, the Force's famed "Musical Ride" has toured Canada, the U.S. and many other countries advertising Canada as a land of Scarlet Tunics and horsemanship. But the Musical Ride is not an accurate representation of who we are and what we do. It does reflect, however, a part of our history and our tradition.

The Royal Canadian Mounted Police, however, is more than Scarlet Tunics and horses. It is also more than a tradition, and it is more than a piece of scarlet cloth. The RCMP is a family. Mounties refer to themselves not as Police Officers but as "Members." As a result, they feel themselves to be not only Police Officers but also members of an extended family. Brothers and sisters bonded together by the clothes they wear, the rules they live by and the oaths they have taken. The time has come for you to meet and better know the family of the modern RCMP. That is why I wrote *Scarlet Tunic.*

My publisher, Art Downs, and I wrestled and searched for a title before we decided on two words: *Scarlet Tunic.* This colorful tunic has remained a tradition which began when the Force was born in 1873 and remains vibrant and alive.

Who are the members of the RCMP? What training do they undergo which molds them into the people they are today? How are their lives different from yours? What secrets do they hold within their 20,000-member family?

These are a few questions that I have attempted to answer in this book. Most of my Brothers and Sisters in this Force are modest — not wanting to talk about their greatest accomplishments. Many of us often secretly feel ashamed for some of the deeds we have reluctantly done in the line of duty. As you will learn, we often suffer through many painful lessons which mold us at times into "Fighters," even though our first duty is as "Peace Keepers." Yes, at times we are violent. The reason is that we face violence and must protect you and ourselves, but we are not happy with violence. Many of us wear scars you will never see — scars inflicted by seeing too much death and not enough life. Scars that have resulted in a very high rate of suicide, alcoholism and divorce on our members.

No one can truly understand what it is like to be a Police Officer. Few people, fortunately, will ever learn what it is like to be beat up, spit on and to experience the happiness and sadness not found in the average occupation. Policemen experience these occurrences on a weekly basis. Some, almost daily. No, we are not asking for your pity. That is not why I wrote *Scarlet Tunic*. I and my Brothers and Sisters just want you to know who we are, to welcome you into our family, and to reassure you that your safety is our primary concern.

We try to uphold over 125 years of tradition. For that, we are quietly proud, even though we shun publicity. This book is not about me. While most of the incidents are those which I have been dispatched to, this book is about my Brother and Sister Officers, family with whom I have shared an abundance of tears and laughter.

Scarlet Tunic is truth, not fiction. Names, however, have been changed to protect the guilty. The innocent do not need protection. Although I have compressed several weeks into 12 hours, all of the incidents happened. This book follows a group of today's Mounties through a 12-hour night shift on Uniform Patrol in Surrey, B.C. Like all of Canada's major communities, this city is multi-cultured with a variety of problems. During this 12-hour shift you will be with members of the RCMP as they respond to calls with consequences from fights with drunks and drug abusers and into homes of normal people caught up in not-so-normal circumstances.

Few people know what happens in the privacy of police cellblocks and the police station, and what happens when a Police Officer is called upon to attend a Crib Death. Mounties do not talk about such experiences to the public. The reason is unclear. It is not distrust. It is not shame. It is not because we do not want you to know. Indeed, we want you to peek inside our lives, to ride inside our cars and to see inside our hearts. Perhaps by accompanying us on patrol you will better understand us — even come to know us as friends.

Scarlet Tunic will take you on a journey for a lost boy, let you see inside our Training Academy, and teach you procedures we use to defend ourselves against an attacker, or attackers. It will bare the souls of the men and women who must attend a house where a child has suddenly and inexplicably died and there is no easy answer and no happy outcome. Yet inside this house of tragedy you will share with us the magic of love and healing.

Scarlet Tunic is not a tale of the "dark side" of life or Police Officers. It is an honest story that will openly show you not only what your Police Officers encounter, but how they deal with the stress they experience. This book is an accurate narrative that will show you how we have learned to accept the unacceptable — and survive in a world that is foreign to most people.

I have been a member of the RCMP for 27 years. As already mentioned, pride is something we seldom publicly admit to, but I am proud to be a member of this Force. I am proud of the men and women I have worked with, and I am proud that the Brother and Sister Officers I work with are my friends. There is a bond which unites us.

With very few exceptions, a Police Officer will face near-certain death to save the life of a fellow officer. We have a sense of belonging, and a sense of duty that the public rarely understands. Why doesn't the public understand? The reason is simply that we do not talk of it openly.

The time has come for this silence to change. Forgive me if I mention again that I am proud, but I am. I am not just proud of the day-to-day duties, dangers and trials I see my fellow officers face but I am proud of their commitment to their duty — to you!

For instance, early in 1994 our Federal Government, as a financial cost-saving measure, decided to freeze the pay scales of all junior members of the Force. In protest, a meeting was held in Surrey, B.C. An astonishing 1,000 Police Officers attended. One of the topics of discussion was plans for "job action" should the Federal Government take away the wages which they had already promised.

"We can plan just about any job action we like, but let's make sure we do not sacrifice our service to the public," was a comment that came from the floor. Senior management was not allowed to attend this portion of our meeting. The words were spoken by a Constable — the lowest rank in our Force.

Boots were stomped and hands clapped in agreement. The protesters decided that no matter what our Government should decide to do, we would never respond by decreasing our response to public need.

I know of few public or private organizations, professional or otherwise, with a commitment to duty that would equal that expressed by 1,000 RCMP officers who attended that late-night meeting.

Having said this, I would like to tell you that Scarlet Tunic is also about you, whom we have sworn to serve. We are your neighbours and friends. We live next door to many of you and we have been to many of your homes, both on and off duty. Usually, time does not allow us to get to know you as well as we would like. I hope, however that *Scarlet Tunic* will correct this problem and provide the opportunity for you to meet our family at your leisure.

Choose a quiet place and an open heart while I introduce you to my Brothers and Sisters — the Modern Mounties.

PROLOGUE

THE TEST

Even a fool, when quiet —
Appears WISE

ROYAL CANADIAN MOUNTED POLICE
TRAINING ACADEMY, REGINA, SASKATCHEWAN

Corporal Don Withers stood tall in front of a class of 32 Royal Canadian Mounted Police recruits. He had entered the class quietly, walked to the podium and slowly and purposely closed the blue and gold binder which held his lesson plan.

The faces in the class were young, fresh and eager, all dreaming of the day they would wear their cherished Scarlet Tunic and accept their badge from the academy's Commanding Officer. Today was different.

"I have one last class to spend with you." He addressed the young faces collectively. "Read your 'Statutes and Regulations,' pages 213 through 237, tonight and you'll all pass your exams. Today, however, I would like to tell you all a story, not just any story — it's my story. At the end, there will be an exam."

The instructor paused, drew in a deep breath and began:

"William Calvert was a decent law-abiding man and he held his high-powered hunting rifle squarely at my chest.

"One hour earlier he had telephoned the police office and calmly declared he would shoot the first officer he saw. If he did not see one within two hours, he would go hunting for his wife and her lover — and shoot them! I was the first police officer he saw.

"I didn't want to die.

"Sergeants are rumored to know everything and the Sergeant on duty at the time had taken advantage of his newly acquired state of omniscience and ordered us not to attend the Calvert residence. The Sergeant's orders were clear and concise. "He'll sober-up and change his mind. Leave him alone."

"There was only one fault in his logic: William Calvert was not drunk. He was suicidal and wanted the police to help him with his final exit.

" 'To Protect and To Serve.' That was our sworn duty. To do so, however, I had to disobey the Sergeant's orders. A very serious offense in the RCMP. But I saw no alternative. While my partner threw a rock through the kitchen window as a distraction, I entered through the front door and quickly found the hallway to the kitchen. I was not prepared to meet Death head-on in someone else's house, but I did.

"Like a phantom, the shape of a man holding a gun calmly appeared in the darkness. He spoke. 'You're a dead man.'

"I froze.

" 'I said you're a dead man,' the voice emphasized.

" 'I know.' I told the truth.

"Calvert reached out with his left hand, turned on the lights and steadied his rifle. In the light he could see that I had already drawn my service revolver. We were standing three feet apart, sharing the view of each other's gun.

" 'Yours is bigger than mine.' I forced a smile.

" 'And it's gonna hurt a lot more, too, when I pull the trigger,' he replied.

"As the seconds passed I looked into the eyes of my executioner, expecting to see the anger of a madman bent on destruction. I did not. Eyes tired from crying mirrored a soul in torment. It was a soul that did not want to kill; it was a soul that wanted to die.

"In the silence our eyes met for a few seconds that stretched into eternity.

"I could take him out with one shot, I thought. If only my hand wasn't shaking so badly. At this distance a headshot is a real possibility ... he'd drop hard ... but if I missed?

" 'Go ahead.' He motioned with his rifle. 'Make your move.'

"Calvert's eyes were red. His cheeks were still wet with tears and his voice said 'I'm sorry' even if his words did not.

"Slowly I holstered my gun. A gamble was about to take place. A wager with two lives being the ante.

" 'Bad script.' I spoke quietly and looked at the floor.

" 'What?'

" 'I don't like the way this movie goes down, Bill. We both die and my wife doesn't even get a pension.'

" 'You got a wife?'

" 'Ya.'

" 'I don't ... anymore.'

" 'I'm sorry.' My eyes teared and the floor became a blur.

" 'No one's ever said that before.' William Calvert, the perpetrator, became Bill — a very lonely man as he laid his gun carefully on the linoleum.

"Somewhere in the silence we met. We understood each other and became friends.

"The following month Bill appeared before a judge, plead guilty to the charge of Pointing a Firearm, and accepted a suspended sentence conditional upon seeking psychiatric help.

"I received an official reprimand for 'Disobeying a Direct Order.' The reprimand would stay on my discipline file for the remainder of my service."

He turned to the cadets, dried his eyes and pretended to be unemotional. "This is your last day at the academy. Tomorrow you will all graduate; however, your homework tonight is to decide if my actions ... these actions I have described to you were correct. Any questions?"

"How long are we supposed to spend on this problem, Corporal?" a chubby cadet called Norman Lumchuck asked.

"The rest of your life!" Corporal Withers shouted. "Before you leave my class...." He pointed a stubby finger that looked more threatening than any gun I had ever seen.

He repeated, "Before you leave my class you had better learn one thing: this Police Academy is of little value except to teach you to march, salute and run 'till you drop in your own vomit. Your real education begins when we give you bullets for your gun and a fast car, then turn you loose on them poor people."

His finger swung horizontally and pointed out the window. "If you are to survive, forget about your bullshit Red Tunic, your high-brown boots and Stetson. They belong on a postcard. To survive, you must learn that life as a cop is a series of lessons and you had better be damned good students."

His short thick finger swung back and forth as he selectively picked us all out individually.

"In this class we have a troop of 32 would-be police officers." Corporal Wither's voice became quiet. After swallowing hard, he offered, "Live each day as if it were the last day of your life because in the next twenty-five years, five of you will be correct. Five of you fine men will be handing in your homework assignment to an instructor much higher in rank than Corporal." His eyes looked up to the ceiling. He was tired. "Now get out of here."

We filed out of the room quietly.

The following summer, Corporal Don Withers was killed on duty.

18

CHAPTER ONE

Sixteen Years Later
THE BRIEFING

*If you don't know where
you're going, you can
never get lost.*

"So life is just a series of lessons, each one building on the other, until the day comes when you sit your final exam. That is the day you will learn the true meaning of a pass/fair grade!"

It had been 16 years since I heard Corporal Withers speak those words. They were words that carried me through hours of boredom and crisis, beautiful sunsets and sunrises, and sometimes through an occasional birth and all-too-many deaths.

The final exam had not yet come for me, but the memory of a man who helped to shape my life kept me wondering: "When, if not today?"

"Hey, Goof, you gonna take notes or just sit there and breathe?"

My mind was jerked back to the present. It was 6:00 p.m. Roll Call. The other police officers in the briefing room laughed as I spoke a short apology to Sergeant Schlitz who was sitting at the head of the table. "Sorry, Sarge."

"I'll see you in my office after briefing!"

The laughing stopped.

Memories of past lessons and Corporal Withers faded away as I opened my black, soft-covered notebook. Like a good cop I began to record a near-endless list of cars and people to "bolf" which meant simply to "Be On the Lookout For." Each briefing offered descriptions of stolen vehicles, major crimes and missing people who had been reported in the past 24 hours. In the next 24 hours we would be tasked with the responsibility of taking calls, arresting drunks, attending family disputes and bolfing. Bolfing was the hardest. It meant your eyes could never rest.

6:15 p.m. Briefing terminated and 23 police officers paraded out the door to the parking lot. Here they loaded their police cars with briefcases, canvas duty bags, shotguns, flashlights, batons, brown-bag lunches and prayers for a safe shift.

I, on the other hand, was privileged to be an honored guest of

Sergeant Schlitz. I was to receive a good reaming-out. I walked into the Watch Commander's office. Sergeant Schlitz sat at his desk, reviewing files from the previous shift. I lowered my eyes in a gesture of defeat. He expected that.

"Close the door!" He looked up over his reading glasses and motioned me to sit at the desk in front of him. Schlitz's office was graced with bullet-proof glass on three sides. It was like sitting in a fishbowl.

"You got a problem?"

"No, sir," I answered.

"Well, I do!" He raised his voice loud enough to penetrate the thick glass and attract the attention of four complaint takers, three radio dispatchers, and the police service dog begging for treats in the dispatch center. The police dog showed his teeth in response to the aggression he sensed in the fish bowl.

"It's okay, Smokey." Tom, the handler, stroked his four-legged companion's head and offered him a small piece of cheese. I could not hear what he said next, but those big brown dog-eyes stared at the Sergeant as though he was being offered up as his next snack. Tom winked at me and turned his back. He respected my privacy.

Then Sergeant Schlitz started. "I got this problem with a certain know-it-all police officer who was daydreaming during my briefing."

He used the words "I" and "My" as weapons during the public execution he was conducting.

"Man — you were light years away! How can I run a briefing when everything I say bounces off the walls? What were you thinking of? Woman? Beer? Let me guess, your girl friend missed her last period ... right?"

"Sarge, I've been happily married for 15 years."

"So your girl friend did miss her period then!"

"No."

"Then what?"

I tried to tell him about Corporal Withers. But when it came to the part where Withers was killed on duty, my throat dried up and my eyes revealed a weakness I did not want my boss to see. Weakness was not allowed on his watch. Only discipline and self-control.

"You got a problem go see the department Shrink. In the meantime, Son," his voice softened ever-so-slightly, "get out there and go to work." He turned his back to me and resumed reading crime reports.

I rose from the chair and walked silently toward the door.

"Hey," Schlitz turned and called out. "Stay sharp. If I see you getting soft on me I'll...." He left his threat unfinished as he motioned me to leave. I again started for the door.

"Just a minute." Schlitz tore a page from a green-lined pad, scratched a few words quickly and folded the page. He pulled a manila envelope from a drawer and slid the page inside. As he licked the flap closed I could read the words "Confidential - Protected A" on the front.

"Take this." He held out the envelope. "Read it before you go off shift. Now go." His voice was still soft and I did not understand why.

"Go!" He motioned me to leave.

I walked down the hall and turned left at a window marked EVERYTHING REQUIRES A SIGNATURE. I signed out a shotgun, portable radio and a set of car keys. The portable fitted snugly into my canvas bag and the shotgun rested between the canvas handles. I left the building as fast as I could.

The parking lot was nearly empty. I opened the trunk of my patrol car, slid the shotgun from its resting place and threw my cloth bag into the trunk. I slammed the lid hard.

A quick walk-around revealed no new "dents of unknown origin" which I could be held accountable for and I opened the passenger door. The only partner I would have tonight was my briefcase. It buckled easily onto the front passenger seat. I swung the passenger door hard. It banged closed.

Standing beside an open driver's door, I loaded the shotgun and reached inside to unlock the rack. A small hidden toggle switch controlled the metal restraint and as I slid the barrel carefully into the blast cup I silently prayed it would not have to come out tonight. Mechanically, I reached out and threw the gate closed on the gun and it locked into place.

The ritual "beginning of shift" continued. I slid into the seat, pulled the steering wheel toward me, cursed the short-legged female who drove the car on day watch and slammed the door. Without thinking, I pushed the seat back a few inches and pulled the seat belt into place.

"It's funny," I thought, "seat belts don't save lives. They just make it easier for paramedics to find the body!" I knew that seatbelts had saved more lives than all the cops in the world, but this was the beginning of a 12-hour night shift and my cynicism was already taking over.

The ignition key turned easily and the engine started with only a slight argument. An array of yellow buttons lit up on the police radio. My finger pushed CLR and RTT. These buttons would signal our dispatcher that my status was "clear and ready to respond." RTT sent another computer message over the airways, lighting up the dispatcher's screen with the message "5 B 23 — Request To Talk."

"KSSHHHT." The radio squelched, signaling someone in the communications center had keyed their microphone.

"5 Bravo 23, acknowledged. You are 10-8. Go ahead."

"5 Bravo 23, mileage is two eight nine seven five, this vehicle 10-8 zone 2 until zero six hundred hours. Am I clear?"

"10-4 Bravo 23. I have Bravo six and thirteen out at a family fight in your zone. No back-up requested."

"10-4."

"Bravo 23?" A quiet female voice whispered from the dispatcher's office. I recognized it as Sharon's.

"Bravo 23."

"Meet me on local Tact."

I reached down and spun the dial to channel five. Tactical was a channel reserved for special operations activities. Our Special Weapons Assault Team claimed it as their personal property every time they went hunting. Their name, S.W.A.T., unofficially came about many years ago when a police officer in the United States referred to a perpetrator as "cockroach." Swatting then became the activity and S.W.A.T. were the men we called.

When it was not being reserved for our specialized teams, Tactical channel was our car-to-car private channel where we often discussed where to meet for coffee, who arrested the biggest drunk that night and other important matters. Usually the Watch Commander turned down his monitor unless a serious matter needed his direction and wisdom.

"23 on Tact. What's up?"

"Have a good time in the fish bowl?" Sharon's voice taunted.

"It was that obvious?"

"Ya. What was that all about?"

"Just the Sarge practicing his control over us." I had used "us." It sounded less personal than "me."

Sharon's voice whispered. "Whatever you told him, sure hurt him bad."

"10-9?" I asked her to repeat.

"He's smoking again. Haven't seen him light up in over two years. A few minutes ago he looked at me through the window ... his face was glazed over like a honey-doughnut. We all ... whoops, gotta go...."

Tact channel went dead.

I doubted it was anything I had said to the boss. He was a man in control. He controlled the radio room dispatchers, he controlled us and he controlled himself. No weakness was ever allowed into his world.

"Bravo 23?" Sharon's voice was changed now. More formal. She called my car number clear and crisp over the dispatch channel.

I responded normally. "Bravo 23, go ahead."

"Sarge was just in the comm-center. Says he'd like to see you at watch-end."

I remained silent.

"Copy last message two-three?"

"10-4. Will do." I was puzzled. Ol' Schlitz demanded, ordered and directed his men. I had never known him to "like to see" anyone. He ordered us to see him.

I cradled the microphone, pulled into traffic and drove off into the same red sunset that all my childhood cowboys had used for their shift-end. Only later was I to learn that my reference to the death of Corporal Don Withers was what had upset rock-hard Sergeant Schlitz.

"Damn!" I swore out loud. After the reaming-out I had received from Schlitz, the sealed envelope I was afraid to open and the puzzled "request" to see him at watch-end, I had totally forgotten about THE DECK.

I looked at my silent, tattered leather partner sitting in the passenger seat. My briefcase.

Automatically I signaled a right turn and pulled into the parking lot of an all-night convenience store. I looked upwards at the neon sign, "7-11". The numbers were supposed to be lucky. I smiled a crooked smile as the truth shoved itself into my mind. We called the 24-hour corner stores convenience marts because they were always open for the convenience of pukes, hypes and any other shit-head with a gun. After his fourth armed robbery in as many weeks, our watch had bought Jim Bretton, the proprietor, a small sign to place over his cash register:

"NO SHOES, NO SHIRT, NO GUN — NO SERVICE!"

After the fifth robbery it was no longer funny. Five robberies in five weeks and Inspector Craig would not authorize a stake-out. Briefly, I recalled the conversation in his office.

"A 24-hour surveillance would cost me over $2,000 in overtime expenditure for just one week! That's bullshit!" Inspector Craig's answer was simple and final. "They're only getting a $100 or $200 each time they hit his store. I'm not about to spend 10 times that amount just to catch a few small-time pukes. Your request for a surveillance is denied." He handed me back my report and photos and his voice softened ever-so-slightly. "It's a shame but I just won't do it."

The Inspector threw the photos we had given him across his table. One of them slid onto the floor. I reached down, picked it up and looked at it. Proprietor Jim was standing behind the counter, pointing to a hole. The masked shopper had pumped two .12-gauge holes into the wall just seconds before he ran out the door and cloaked himself in the night's darkness.

"Yes, Sir, it's a shame all right." I could feel the words being funneled from my brain to my mouth but I couldn't stop them. "I'll tell Jim and his wife that until their losses exceed the cost, we won't protect his life."

Inspector Craig leaned forward on his desk. "I don't like your attitude!" The worst thing that could ever happen to a Mountie was for an officer "not to like your attitude."

I leaned forward, invaded his newly-expanded body space and returned his glare. Clearly he could see that I did not like his attitude, either.

"Is that all, sir?" I became the aggressor.

Inspector Craig leaned back, once again established a safe distance and a new body space.

"If I didn't have all these crime statistics, man-hour sheets and damned audits on my desk, I'd be out there with you!" His eyes swung tiredly, surveying the mounds of paper stacked randomly on his desk.

"Tell Jim I'm sorry. If I don't stick to my budget, they'll transfer in someone who will. That won't solve any problems. It seems I'm working for a boss who gets a Christmas bonus for the money I save him. Some days life sucks!" He looked down sadly. "I wish I could help ... but my hands are tied."

"I'll tell him that — exactly, Sir." I softened my approach. "He won't understand, but then I guess you and I don't either."

Inspector Craig looked at me sadly as I turned to leave his office. I quietly walked through his door, wondering what had happened to a once-good-cop.

As I approached the 7-11 I got ready to park the police car. Instinct guided me to a parking stall where I could safely see inside the store yet still maintain physical cover. I was doing a lot of things these days by instinct and I often wondered if I was becoming a good cop ... or just a cop.

Then my thoughts jerked back to the present. No daydreaming was allowed inside a police car. Not if I was to be a good cop. But I had a problem. The reaming-out I had received from Sergeant Schlitz interrupted the ritual I had observed at the beginning of every shift for the past 16 years.

At the beginning of each shift I played a game — THE DECK. It was a game of chance and a game of memories. More important, it was a way I could keep a promise and salute the memory of a man who had walked into my world and changed its direction. He had also saved my life in many ways, but I could not save his.

He was my Regina instructor, Corporal Don Withers.

Reaching into my briefcase, I fingered a worn deck of cards. As I retrieved the Deck, I watched the endless parade of customers enter and leave Jim's store and allowed my mind to drift back through the years to Regina's R.C.M.P. Recruit Training Academy where boys usually became men and women often became bitter.

The Police Academy, appropriately called "DEPOT," was truly a stopover for young police cadets who would learn all they could about life, law and control. It was a place where they would bake sun-dry under the hot summer prairie sun and experience the stabbing chill of frostbitten ears and fingertips in December.

For most cadets, however, the only memories that would remain would be the ramrod discipline and the pride in something called a "Scarlet Tunic."

It was December. Our six-month training was at the half-way mark and we were all eagerly waiting for five days leave. Our Commanding Officer had promised us all a short vacation wherein we would be allowed to go home for Christmas. It was to be a dream come true. A short visit with parents and girl friends. Just enough time to allow us to steep ourselves in a painful disease we secretly admitted to: Homesickness!

Mid-December! A time of exams, troop marching in sub-zero prairie winds and dreams of Christmas at home.

I was in the gymnasium working my way to the minimum 125 pounds of iron that I would have to raise over my head in order to graduate. The silver bar balanced 60 pounds of metal on either end and stubbornly refused to rise past my chin. In disgust, I let the weights slam into the floor in an attention-arousing clang that announced my failure to all the other recruits nearby.

"Apologize, young man!"

I spun around. Corporal Withers was standing at the door. "I said apologize!" In five or six long strides, he had walked 20 feet and stationed himself only inches from my face.

"I'm sorry, Corporal!" I shouted my apology and snapped to attention.

"Not to me you Idiot!"

I looked around the room. Thirty-one recruits were watching. All movement had stopped. The gym was dead-quiet. Corporal Withers was an academic instructor. His presence in the gym was exceptionally strange. Why was he here? What did he have to do with weight training? Withers was in charge of our minds — our bodies had been handed over to sadistic pain-loving gorilla cops who took strange delight in inflicting injury in the name of manhood. Withers was too nice a man to walk through the gates of Hell, into a gymnasium stained with spit, vomit and blood.

"Apologize to who?" I was embarrassed.

Withers spun his bony finger-weapon around the gymnasium to the other cadets in our troop. "To them! You're a weakling! If you don't get that bloody bar over your head, they'll graduate as a troop of 31! Do you know how stupid a troop of 31 looks on the parade square?" He shouted and it echoed off the walls of Hell.

I shook my head.

"The Commanding Officer is already having a sign painted. It's a big sign. We always make big signs for little boys like you! Do you know what it says? Don't answer. I'll tell you. It says: 'This troop has 31 graduates because Teather was too weak! Teather gave up! Teather doesn't care! Teather wasn't, isn't and never will be a man'!"

Withers motioned for two cadets to add another 20 pounds to the bar.

"Now you reach down, grab that pissy-assed bar and you jerk it up so hard it'll make orbit!"

I reached down and gripped the bar squarely. Anger was all I could feel. Anger and rage. Emotions so violent I did not care about graduating. I did not care about Corporal Withers and I didn't even care about the bar.

"One more thing you dozy little boy."

I gripped the bar harder.

"You jerk that bar up or I'll personally add 'FAGGOT' to the sign and send it home to your Mother!"

All the humiliation I had ever suffered channeled itself through my body. Somewhere inside, an explosion propelled the barbell up over my head and, as my arms straightened, success numbed the pain.

Somewhere, lost in rage, my mind faintly heard my troop screaming. My troop. Screaming — yelling — cheering.

CHEERING!

The iron hit the floor, bounced over and died in defeat.

Withers smiled. Quietly he spoke. "In your greatest weakness, you will find infinite strength." Then he added. "You stink! Hit the showers and report to the parade square. You got 10 minutes."

Police cadets are taught to do everything fast. We had learned to eat, march, think and even shower double-time. In seven minutes the winter prairie air was freezing my still-wet hair. I marched double-time to a single dark shadow which stood death-still in the center of the parade square. It was waiting for me.

"Reporting as ordered, Corporal!" I stopped three feet in front of Withers and jerked to attention. The warm pride I had felt after defeating the iron bar was still pumping through my veins. By contrast, the sharp biting night wind had frozen everything in sight — except me and Corporal Withers.

I can still remember how he looked up at the stars that night. Still and quiet. A black shadow against star-lit snow. It was like a phantom or a faint memory from a childhood dream.

"Just think." He held his gaze skyward. "These are the same stars that shone on the Roman Centurions."

"Huh?"

"The Roman Centurions. The original Peace Officers. Ever wonder how they did it? How they kept law and order?" He gave me no time to respond. "They had discovered the magic ratio! The ratio was one police officer, one Centurion to guard over 500 civilians. Did you know that?"

I shook my head.

"It was the Romans. They played with ratios — finally settled on what we call 'Grave's Constant'!"

"Grave's Constant?"

"Grave's Constant. Too many police officers and the government becomes too powerful and civilians become persecuted, oppressed. Oppressions means civilians die." He looked over to a small monument on the edge of the parade square. "And too many civilians and we lose control. We also lose cops, good cops! Too many graves either way. That's why we call it 'Grave's Constant'! The perfect balance to keep the graves to a minimum is one police officer — one Centurion for every 500 civilians. Five hundred to one!"

"Then why has our Force adopted a nation-wide ratio of 1,000 to one. Are we twice as good?" My young eager mind parroted the words it had been taught were true.

"No, my friend. Our Force is twice as stupid. Look, young man, this whole idea of us Mounties being Canada's Finest is just so much bullshit! What you got is a dose of Scarlet Fever!"

"Scarlet Fever?" I asked. I had heard that phrase used to describe the many tourist girls who visited Regina, hoping to hook up with a young Mountie. We referred to them kindly as having Scarlet Fever. In the privacy of our barracks, however, they were known as 'The Ditch Pigs From Hell'!

"Scarlet Fever, Corporal? But that's for the girls."

"No, it's not! I've been instructing at this academy for nearly three years. I'm about to be shipped out this spring. What I see here is a horrible communicable disease. Scarlet Fever! And you, my friend, have one of the worst cases I've ever seen. You got this disease so bad that 15 minutes ago you were more prepared to dislocate both shoulders than be embarrassed in front of your own troop!

"Oh, Scarlet Fever ain't always bad ... once in a while, a rare while, it brings out our good points such as honesty, strength and resolve; but it can be fatal." Withers walked slowly over to the small cairn and placed his hand on the memory of the many "good cops" who had lost their lives in the performance of their duty. I followed him.

"I'm sorry." I looked down at my feet.

"Don't apologize. We are the ones responsible. Since the first day you arrived here at Mountie Birthing Center we've told you that you are the best. Soon you will believe it and you'll march down this parade square with a complete troop of 32 men, each one believing he is indestructible."

He paused, wiped the corner of his eye and looked at the names on the cairn. "Then one dark night you, or one of your troop-mates, will walk straight into a bullet — maybe from your own gun!" Corporal Withers was not making up a story — he was telling one.

My mind raced ahead. We had always looked on Corporal Withers as our Master. He had seen and done it. His tales of wrestling drunken Indians on reservations, high-speed car chases and shoot-outs had always kept us awake in class. Withers was the only academic instructor we'd seen who taught lessons out of the book he called "Life." Many instructors were sent to Depot as a punitive three-year cooling off sentence. Their crimes were usually crimes of violence — often alcohol-related.

But Withers, our troop hero, was now telling me one of us could eat his own gun?

"Suicide?" I turned to clarify his message.

"What was the first task we had you complete when you arrived here last September?"

"I dug a grave in our cemetery." I recalled that duty clearly. The measurements were exact and the walls vertical. Perfectly vertical.

"Suicide." He spoke the word quietly and clearly.

"Too many graves." He shook his head. "If you learn nothing else from this academy my young brother, I want you to learn this." Withers looked me in the eye. He seemed so wise, so tall and for the first time I had noticed — so compassionate.

"Some things never change." I quietly suggested. Staring at the cairn I remembered the grave I had dug.

"No, not that. Things that shouldn't change ... like the stars, good friendships and ..." His words trailed off.

"And these." He reached deep into his pea-jacket pocket and produced a deck of white cards.

"Twenty-three years ago my best friend and I sat on our beds one night in "C" Block. As a matter of fact, I think we shared the same dormitory as you. We were feeling sort of down at the time. Graduation was one week away and we were going to be posted over 4,000 miles apart."

"Well, he and I cut out 106 white cards." He held the deck like an old friend would hold his last will and testament. "Then we split them into 53 cards each. On each card we wrote a message ... a truth, something that would remind us of each other. Fifty-two bits of truth.

"After we finished, we handed each other our deck. We made a pact. A solemn promise that at the beginning of every shift we would draw a card, read the message and remember our friendship. The message would follow us throughout the shift and be our silent partner. If we were really stumped, we could draw a card anytime — for help, advice or just to salute an old friendship. The two decks that we shared would ensure that we would never be alone."

"I'm not sure I understand."

"Here. Let me show you how this Magic Deck works. I watched you trying to lift 120 pounds over your head just 30 minutes ago. You couldn't! As I watched you from the doorway, I pulled out the Deck, cut it once and read the top card."

He turned over the card from the Deck and held it out at eye level for me to read:

In your greatest weakness;
You will find infinite strength.

I saw your weakness. It was fear. Fear of failure, fear of humiliation and fear of that monster anger that you keep caged inside you. Did you know that your self-defense instructor fears you?"

"Fritz? The Maniac?" I bit my lip and apologized. "He has a black belt in everything! Even threatened to kill us all with a rolled-up newspaper once! How could he fear me? He's the killer, not me!"

"Corporal Leitz says you're like a python at a Hamster convention. Once you get started, you eat everything in sight! He once told us that when you start to fight, you frost all over and your face looks like a double-glazed honey doughnut. You don't stop 'till your opponent runs or lies still."

"I'm not that bad ... am I?"

"Ever lost a fight?"

"No."

"For 151 pounds I'd say you've done remarkably well then! But your anger ... your rage ... it might just turn on you some day. Think on that! Anger can be a horrible weakness."

I reached down inside myself and saw a dark figure so hideous I looked away. "And the card?" I asked.

"Well," Corporal Withers continued, "the card reminded me that if we could channel our weaknesses and guide them, they might become our greatest strength. Your anger, rage and fear of humiliation allowed you to raise 140 pounds of iron clear over your head. Five minutes earlier you couldn't even raise 120 pounds up to your chin."

I looked at the deck of cards that had just guaranteed I would graduate with my troop.

"Tomorrow I'll sign you off at the 140-pound mark. You can stop worrying about failure now."

"The Deck did that?" I asked.

"The Deck." Withers acknowledged. He held it like a pet. "It has other powers, too. Strange, wonderful, magic powers."

"Oh? Like what?"

"You'll find out. Here, take it!"

Don held out the Deck for me to hold. I briefly fanned through the cards. Twenty-three years of use had rendered some of the cards bent, torn and, a few, stained and sticky. One card I had noticed quickly was unlike the others. It was thick. I pulled it from the Deck. It was blank. Holding it up to Wither's face, I asked, "The Joker?"

He smiled and wiped the corner of his eye.

"No, that's a special card. We each wrote one special message, glued another card just around the edges so it could be removed, and placed it on top. We placed our sealed cards in each other's Deck. That single sealed card contains a message for the Deck holder. It can be opened and read only once."

I wondered why, in 23 years, Don had never opened this secret.

"When would this card be opened?" I asked, hoping for an answer my young mind could comprehend.

"You'll know when to look!"

"Me? I ... but these cards are yours!"

"They never were mine. Only the memory of my troop-mate and the friendship we shared is mine. In two years I'll be retiring ... won't need them anymore. Part of our promise was to see that if we ever retired ... or died ... these cards would live on. They are now yours — but I shall miss them dearly."

I looked into the tired eyes of my Master. He was giving me the greatest possession he had ever owned and I did not know why. I thought I would look for the answer in the Deck.

Carefully, I shuffled and cut the Deck. I turned the top card over and read:

The best mirror
is found in
The eyes of a friend.

I looked quietly into the eyes of Corporal Don Withers. He was 43 years old going on 90. For a moment I wondered what had aged him so, but he had somehow read my mind and cut my thoughts short.

"You'll find out soon enough." He continued. "Bob — please take these cards — I fear they have more miles on them than I have left on me. Use them wisely. Start each shift with a card and let the card guide you as it has guided me. Use them to help you through the tough times, for they have the ability to do just that."

"But these are ... these cards are...."

"These cards are now yours. I only ask one favor of you."

"Anything. It's yours!"

"Whenever you consult the Deck ... remember me ... please?"

Deep inside, my guts twisted and tightened. I felt an emotion I had never felt before and I wasn't sure what it was. It hurt. It felt good. I wanted to laugh, to cry, to scream to the stars that I had just found a friend. I wanted to quietly whisper an oath to a new-found friend.

Quietly I promised. "I will."

What happened next was both confusing and frightening for a police cadet. I had removed my glove and extended my hand. It was a manly thing to do when making a promise, especially to a superior officer.

Corporal Withers looked at my naked hand for just a second. Then I caught a glance coming from the face of a friend. A glance that was foreign, scary and everything all-at-once. Withers took three steps forward and threw his arms around me. The strength this man possessed was mixed with the gentleness of a friend and I felt both. It was a strange and confusing sensation.

Until that night-under-the-stars, my life had been empty. I had never felt the true strength of raising 140 pounds of iron high in the air, nor had I felt the strength given in the embrace of a friend. And gentleness? Until then I had only known gentleness to be the sign of a coward. Although I didn't know how to return the embrace, I gave it a clumsy attempt.

Somewhere between three seconds and an eternity, two lonely men stepped outside of time and shared the countless stars with a million brave Centurions who had gone before. It was a family that I had joined — a brotherhood unknown to most people. It was a brotherhood rarely shared by members of the same family.

Then — I said goodbye to a friend.

Don refused to use the word goodbye. He referred to it as the "G" word. Instead he would simply say "Adios, Partner," sounding like a cliche out of an old "B" Western movie.

As we parted company that night, we both looked at the stars God had hung in the cold prairie blackness. We saluted our brothers who had gone before us, stood silent for a moment. Then silently, Don

Withers walked away. I was left with a deck of cards, two frost-bitten ears and a memory.

As he disappeared around the corner of "C" Block I cut the deck and read the top card:

Good-byes are a
necessary pause —
Before Good Friends
can meet again.

I never saw Corporal Don Withers again. The following week he was transferred to a small town in Northern Saskatchewan. Six months later, a bullet — fired in anger — tore into his chest and ended his life.

"Adios, Corporal Withers. Adios, Friend."

Corporal's cloth shoulder patch.

CHAPTER TWO

THE MAGIC OF THE DECK

Ignorance has two traps:
Believing what isn't so,
and
Not believing what is.

Depot Training Academy and all its memories faded but my mind failed to let go of Corporal Withers' face. As I slowly cut the Deck, I could still see his face superimposed on the back of each card. I had kept my promise — not to forget him.

I turned over the top card as I had done so many times before. Each card held a new surprise for me and I felt renewed each time I consulted the Deck. I had often thought it interesting, but never fully realized just how magic this Deck had become. Often a familiar card would surface and give me advice — the words were the same as the last time chance had turned the card for me, but my understanding different. Each saying, each truism printed on these cards carried with them the ability to magically transform their meaning to a form I most needed at the time.

Saluting the memory of a man I could never be, I read the top card aloud. Somehow, I believed that if the words that were to guide me for the next 12 hours were empowered by speech, they would be more effective. As I read the card aloud, my eyes studied each word:

Never surrender your
Principles —
Without them,
You are nothing.

Okay. So I had a shotgun, a fast car, a deck of cards and my principles — whatever they were. Not much to guide me through another 12 hours of Hell. But that's all I had.

Principles. A set of rules to live by. Police Officers live, eat and often die for the intangible Principles they swore to uphold. The oaths we took when we were sworn in were easy to remember. They were also easy to translate into every day language:

THE OATH OF ALLEGIANCE

"I do swear that I will be faithful and bear true allegiance to Her Majesty Queen Elizabeth the Second, Queen of Canada, her heirs and successors according to law. So Help Me God."

Translation:
It was easy to swear to bear allegiance to your country and your Queen, although I often wondered how that oath could be applied when I arrested my quota of Friday night drunks or gave out an ordered quota of traffic tickets.

THE OATH OF OFFICE

"I solemnly swear that I will faithfully, diligently and impartially execute and perform the duties required of me as a member of the Royal Canadian Mounted Police, and will well and truly obey and perform all lawful orders and instructions that I receive as such, without fear, favour or affection of or towards any person. So help me God."

Translation:
You will execute your duties without any favour of gain or fear of pain. This meant you could not give a friend a warning for speeding. He received a ticket. It also meant you lost a friend. Fear of pain was also simply translated. You will never give up in a fight until you have won or been beaten unconscious.

I had tried the latter and the sometimes weakness on the left side of my body would often remind me of the temporary paralysis I had received after being clubbed, from behind. I never did find out who it was, but I had kept the oath in a dark wooden area. I had displayed no fear of pain ... until I awoke in a hospital, blind, paralyzed and unable to speak.

THE OATH OF SECRECY

"I do solemnly swear that I will keep absolutely secret all knowledge and information of which I may become possessed through my position with the Royal Canadian Mounted Police; that I will not, without due authority in that behalf, discuss with members of the Force or any other person, either by word or letter, any matter which may come to my notice through my employment with the said Royal Canadian Mounted Police. So help me God."

Translation:
You cannot talk about your work, your investigations or even your problems to anyone except another Police Officer. Your wife was clearly not on the list of people you could confide in. A sad ending,

34

indeed, for all-too-many marriages when this oath was taken seriously.

The Oaths of Office, Allegiance and Secrecy — all clear principles. A bit too simple, perhaps, but we had principles at least. When they wore thin there was whiskey and sleep, the final reward after taking one too many calls on a busy night shift.

As if it could read my thoughts, the police radio came to life.

"Five Bravo 23," it called. I quickly wrapped the cards in an old handkerchief and stuffed them back into my briefcase. I picked up the mike, held it close to my lips and answered: "5 Bravo 23."

"Two-three, clear for a call?" Sharon always shortened her sentences when she was busy.

"Stand-by one." I asked her to wait a second or three.

"Advise when ready," she acknowledged.

I had wrapped the Deck in an old handkerchief, the same one it came wrapped in that cold night on the parade square a long time ago in a distant land. Reaching over to my right, I repositioned them in my briefcase, sat upright and reached into my shirt pocket. Retrieving my notebook, I opened it to a clear page. With my notebook in my left hand, ball point pen in my right, I juggled the microphone.

"Two Three's ready to copy. Go ahead Sharon."

"Two Three, we have a complaint of missing youth. Boy aged six. Name Clarence Henderson. I spell H.E.N.D.E.R.S.O.N. — Stop Check?"

"10-4." I acknowledged that I had copied all the information given so far.

"Continuing. See his parents William and Megan at one-eight-four-nine-three Tolmie Drive. The boy was last seen at seventeen hundred hours, should be in company with his golden retriever, last seen wearing a brown and gray sweat suit. Stop Check?"

"I copy so far. That's a funny way to dress your dog." I tried to add some humor to another routine call.

"See the parents and advise further details when you have them. We'll put the boy on the system when we have enough info. Your file number is eighty-nine dash four-one-six-two-six. Time dispatched is eighteen thirty hours: YOU ARE NOW ASSIGNED CODE 2!" Sharon's voice emphasized her last instruction.

Putting the boy on the system I understood. It meant his name, full description and all other information would be placed on a country-wide computer system. Any police officer checking a boy by the same name on this data-base would instantly be supplied with all the information available. This would be handy if he turned up lost in a neighborhood a couple of miles away. Children often wander, I thought. I sure hope he wanders into Zone Four. Stu's working that area and he was magical around children and old people.

Code 2? Like a delayed response suffered after catching a lightening bolt smack between your eyes, the last words played back in my mind. CODE 2?

Sharon's voice had revealed an uneasiness we did not often hear. Either ol' Schlitz had just asserted his control over her, or she had felt something different in this complaint. I could only guess.

"CODE 2? FOR A MISSING YOUTH?" I spoke the words out loud in disbelief. Code 2 was a response priority second only to Code 3, red lights and siren! Code 2 meant I was to respond immediately, all other calls and duties to be immediately suspended. Why was this call priorized?

I reached over, slid the microphone back into its clip and wedged my open notebook between the shotgun rack and the car radio. It was a small discovery I had made a few weeks prior — my notebook hung open so I could easily refer to the address of my next call. A police officer's brains are always on overload, driving the blue and white, assessing the current call, dodging traffic and BOLFING. Damn, I hated BOLFING!

I pulled out of the parking lot, waved at Jim Breton standing behind the cash register, and returned his thumbs up okay signal. It was his way of saying he hadn't been robbed — today.

Traffic was heavy, even for a Friday evening, but I eased the marked police car into the slow lane, mentally drew a map of the shortest route to Tolmie Drive and turned left at the first no-left-turn sign I could find.

Code 2? For a missing six-year-old? I was still wondering why when I turned hard onto the Henderson's street. Tolmie Drive was a gravel road which cut through a small rural community on the edge of town. In the privacy of our briefing room we referred to this collection of small farms as Mayberry and all of its citizens as Gomers, except the women. They were Gomerettes. But they were nice people. A bit poor by city standards, but decent, honest and hard working. They were friends. Friends to each other and friends to outsiders. I was an outsider. Past calls in this area had shown it to be near impossible to attend a complaint in Mayberry without accepting an obligatory coffee. On occasion, a country thank-you came in the form of a lunch or supper. Tonight there would be no time for a country thank-you. No time for coffee, no time for social chatter about a favorite heifer and no time for anything except taking details and accepting the next call on the police radio.

I pulled into Henderson's driveway. My mind was already busy making excuses. I could clear this call in 10 minutes if I was good. Since it was Friday night, the shops downtown would soon be closing and there would be the usual rush of shoplifters. People will be coming home from work tonight and finding their houses broken into and, as the evening turns to night, there will be the drunks. Ever-entertaining drunks.

I had thrown $5 into the hat at briefing. The usual betting pool was announced and $85 would be split three ways. The three prizes would be awarded to the officer who had arrested the biggest, the drunkest or the most colorful drunk. Tonight, I was going after color and one third of $85 — however much that was. A missing six-year-old wouldn't stop or even slow me down tonight. How wrong we can be!

"Bravo Two-Three, 10-7 last call." I advised the comm-center I would be out of my car.

"Copy Two-Three. Advise please when you have further details."

"10-4." I hung the mike in its silver clip and shut off the engine.

The driveway was hard-packed dirt. Both sides were lined with neatly fitting stones which held together to form two perfectly matching three-foot walls. I ran my hand along the top of the granite jig-saw puzzle and envied the rocks. They were granted the good fortune of fitting in place. I was not. I envied anything orderly and firm in life — goals I had not yet learned to reach.

Mr. Henderson was waiting at the top of the driveway. He was upset. In a few minutes, he would tell me everything I did not want to hear.

His son Clarence was not a wanderer. He was always ready and eager for supper. Today, he was an hour overdue and had not been seen since "sometime just after we fed the chickens," which had been 2:00 p.m.

Clarence was last seen playing near the makeshift wharf which jutted about 10 feet into the Fraser River at the rear of the farm. He and Tillie, his golden retriever, often played at the water's edge. Tillie would locate frogs and Clarence would catch them. It was a game that Meg, Clarence's mother, had invented. When Clarence became bored she would give him a large paper bag and send him down to the river. His mission was simple. Clarence was in charge of Froggery. It was a serious responsibility for a young lad. Just how serious we would soon learn.

Using the paper bag his mother supplied, his mission was to patrol the river and fill it with frogs. When he had collected 12 frogs, he could make a wish and it would come true. Any wish he wanted. It was guaranteed. Clarence knew this to be true and took his frog responsibilities seriously. Every boy knows that a wish empowered by 12 wet green frogs is not a thing to be taken lightly.

There was only one problem. Within the first hour of frog hunting, the wet green hoppers would melt their way through the paper bag and Clarence and Tillie would return home — happy but frogless.

Today he had not come home. I told Clarence's father I'd have a look around.

Walking quietly behind the house, I passed a small duck pond and chicken coop. A path led behind the barn and along the edge of a small meadow, over a rise and down to the river. It was a perfect trail for a young frog hunter to follow. It led to magic lands full of dragons, monsters and escaping frogs. I followed it, trying to remember a childhood — a childhood I had left behind a long time ago in a foggy mist.

Find the frogs and you'll find the boy. I chanted it quietly. In truth I was hoping to hear Tillie barking in the distance. Meg had described the "silly-fit" that Tillie had whenever she was confronted with a herd of runaway frogs.

The wharf was less than 100 yards ahead. What I saw made my heart sink, my throat tighten and the walk seem like an eternity. Fifty feet from the wharf I stopped. Tillie was quietly sitting on the rickety structure, her back toward me.

"Clarence ... Clarence. How's froggin'?" I called out — and waited for a reply.

"Clarence?" I tried again. Louder this time.

Nothing.

Tillie turned around, looked at me then looked out over the river. I knew he had to be somewhere nearby. Tillie was tied to him by a bond stronger than any leash.

I walked out onto the wharf, stopped and reached down to stroke Tillie on her head. I was about to ask her where Clarence had gone but I didn't have to. Her soft golden face refused to look up. Her body trembled with each whine she quietly spoke. In her mouth she held —

A paper bag....

I sat down beside Tillie and held her close. I could feel her body leaning tight next to mine. It was warm and her dog-smell reminded me of my own childhood friend.

She trembled.

A pair of soft dog-eyes looked me square in the face and asked a question I could not answer. Softly, Tillie laid the paper bag in my lap, looked at me again and poked the bag with her nose. Today there would be no frog-chasing, silly-fit for a golden retriever. There would be no squeals of excitement and there would be no weary return home by a six-year-old boy who had discovered a Magic Kingdom, vanquished dragons and lost a dozen wet frogs.

Today, time had stopped.

38

Tillie and I hit the wall together. It hurt.

"It's okay, Tillie. We'll find him." My throat choked. "You never were a good tracker. He's probably over at the Jensen's pond looking for more frogs and you just lost his trail."

Tillie knew I was lying. She knew I could not face the truth. I wasn't strong enough.

The evening sun was warm on our backs as we held each other. I now held Tillie's friendship leash and we looked out over the river, together. The water gurgled as it pushed by the end of the wharf.

GOD — I hated that sound!

The walk back to the Henderson house was the longest journey of my life. I left Tillie sitting on the wharf, looking at the river, and made the trek back alone.

Half-lying to myself, half-lying to Clarence's father, I explained only that "Clarence must be around — somewhere." That fact afforded him some relief, but I knew the relief was only temporary.

In my notebook I collected the usual list of descriptions, time and details. An explanation was offered to the Hendersons. I outlined the procedure I would follow in calling our Police Service Dog and explained that he would be here soon. I asked them both to ensure they took Tillie into the house. Our Police Dog did not like competition.

The paper bag that Tillie had given me was folded flat and tucked beneath my shirt. It crackled as I moved but it was at least concealed — from everyone, except me.

Efficiently and professionally I said my goodbyes and walked to my police car. As I opened the door I remembered how nice it was to visit a neighborhood where locked doors were not necessary. I slid in behind the steering wheel, turned on the ignition, adjusted the squelch on the radio for better reception and paused. In the rear-view mirror I watched Bill and Meg enter their house, not knowing exactly what was happening. Perhaps it was best for now, I thought. Maybe there's a chance. I hoped against all hope.

Reaching down, I pushed a lit button on the radio. An electronic code was sent. "Request to talk."

"5 Bravo 23, go ahead." Sharon was waiting for my call. In short police sentences I relayed all the information I wanted her to hear. Our Police Dog was requested for a land search and I would await his arrival.

"Need anyone else?" Sharon's voice told me she somehow knew what I knew. She was suggesting the services of our Underwater Recovery Team.

Briefly I wrestled with the truth, then denied it.

"Just call Tom ... for now. I'll wait here." I rejected any suggestion that Clarence had drowned. For now, it was a secret to be shared only with Tillie.

"5 Bravo 23, Echo Six is on the way."

"10-4. What's his status?" Echo Six was Tom Haworth's car. He was our senior dogmaster. I liked Tom. He cared. I almost looked forward to seeing him and Smokey, his furry companion.

"He's just leaving the office. Should be there in 15 minutes."

"10-4." I acknowledged. Fifteen minutes sitting in a vacuum can be an eternity. The air inside the car was stale and smelled of sweat and vomit from a drunk the night previous. I stood outside in the warmth of the summer and allowed my mind to take in the summer evening.

Looking toward the West I could see a big orange sun losing its fight against gravity as it was slowly sucked down toward the horizon. Somewhere in the glow of the sunset, a memory drifted by. It was as though the sunset had become a doorway in time and for an infinitely long second I stepped through — back to the Academy and my days as a cadet.

Our police psychologist, Dr. Bayless, stood in front of the class. He looked astute, intellectual, in his dark suit and half-rim reading glasses as he glanced at his notes and looked out over the podium. His four-hour lecture was summed up in thirty seconds.

"Men. If you forget all I have said today, that's okay." He paused for a moment and removed his glasses. "I do, however, want you all to remember that in the life you have chosen as police officers, there are only two rules:

RULE #1: As police officers, you will learn that innocent people often die.

AND

RULE #2: There is absolutely nothing you can do to change Rule #1.

Dr. Bayless folded his lecture notes, stepped down from the podium and quietly left the classroom. There was no applause. Our silence showed a deeper form of respect and awe for what he had taught us that day.

We as quietly filed out of the lecture hall and the memory blurred and faded.

I blinked, bringing myself back to the present and wished for the counsel of a wiser man to help me through this shift.

Like a smoker absent-mindedly reaching for a package of cigarettes, I had walked over to my vehicle, reached in through the open window and retrieved from my briefcase — the Deck.

It was a ritual. I unwrapped the cards, tucked the cloth behind my gunbelt (the paper bag under my shirt crackled), cut the deck and turned over the top card:

> *If Today is the First day*
> *of the rest of your life —*
> *What was Yesterday?*

I was in no mood for humor and, failing to understand the seriousness of the card, I turned over the next one:

> *Your answers lie not*
> *in this deck ...*
> *But in the reason*
> *You consulted it!*

I thought for a minute and pondered the exclamation mark which was supposed to give the card emphasis. Why did I consult the Deck? Was I lonely? Yes. Did I need help? Yes. Was I afraid to look inside myself for answers?

I looked at the next card:

> *You are never given a question*
> *without the ability to answer it.*
> *Every problem carries with it,*
> *its own reward.*

Then I saw, ever so faintly, in pencil, Don had scratched his own answer in the corner:

"Growth."

Like Peter Pan, I wanted to live in Never-Never Land — a place where children never had to grow up. If growth meant pain, then I would choose to remain a child. But I was exiled from Never-Never Land the day I swore three oaths. Now the pain was mine — and the growth — although I was not ready to accept either.

Looking away from my answers I could see, a quarter mile down the gravel road, a cone-shaped cloud. Man and dog were arriving. I wrapped the Deck, placed it back in my briefcase and waved to Tom as he pulled into the driveway.

Smokey was out of the air-conditioned car close behind his Master. They were inseparable. Quietly, they both listened to my story. I loosened two buttons on my shirt and showed them the paper bag. Smokey looked away. I tucked the bag back into my shirt, buttoned it and finished relating what I had seen and where I had walked. The latter was necessary. Tom did not want to waste time tracking me. He and Smokey would begin their search following an older trail — Clarence's.

Who was I kidding. I knew where Clarence's track led.

"Okay. We'll see what we can do."

Tom, the eternal optimist, strayed from his usual character as he looked down and softly said, "Want me to call the Dive Team?"

"No. Not yet." I was looking down at the hard-packed gravel, hoping to find an answer I could live with. Tom reached out, put his hand on my shoulder and looked me in the eyes.

"You okay?" he asked.

"Ya." I lied.

"Bugs you, doesn't it."

"I'll get over it."

"No, you won't." Tom knew the truth. During my career I had served on our Police Dive Team and recovered over 100 bodies of drowning victims. Male, female, adults and children. Every night of my life the faces of the children poked their way into my sleep and dreams became nightmares. The body recoveries would never become routine — nor would the faces of the mothers, fathers, sisters and brothers I faced after each dive. Each body recovery took something from me until one day I found myself empty. Alone.

I knew Tom spoke the truth. I would never get over it.

I turned away, wishing them both good luck and climbed back into the safety of my police car.

"C'mon, Smokey. Let's go find us some frogs," I heard Tom say as he and his best friend walked toward the rear of the house.

"And a six-year-old boy named Clarence ... please God ... make it so." I prayed the words out loud.

Ignition on, car in gear, easy on the accelerator. Not nice to throw the Henderson's gravel around. I pulled out of the driveway, turned left on Tolmie and drove off into the sunset and away from Never-Never Land.

I was growing up.

Cloth emblem worn by members of the Police Dog Service Section.

CHAPTER THREE

BATMAN, REDMAN AND WOLFE CREEK BRIDGE

Things are more like they
are now —
Than they have ever been
before.

"COMPARTMENTALIZE!" Cut it up into little pieces. Keep each piece in its own separate room and only visit one room at a time! I could almost see the advice written on the windshield of my police car. It was like a heads-up display used in fighter jets. I could read the words and still see the road. The sentences once spoken to a room crammed full of wide-eyed police cadets now played across my windshield. As each sentence faded into road dust, one simple word kept reappearing:
COMPARTMENTALIZE!

That was the secret to mental health that we had been taught in training. Somehow the words from our police psychologist had followed me for 16 years. They echoed in the privacy of my car and I could still hear the voice from our training academy at Regina — a place far far away and a long time ago.

"As Police Officers," I clearly recalled Dr. Bayless saying, "you must be many people. Each one separate and distinct from the other. At home you must be a loving parent, husband or wife — but once you put on your gun and walk out the door you will allow yourself to be transformed into many people! To a drunk, you must appear firm, jovial and parent-like. At your thousandth house break-in, you must appear interested. Even if you don't care anymore 'cause you know you'll never find the bastard that raped their home! At a family fight — your third one of the night — you must appear like you really give a shit."

We all laughed.

"And when confronted by an assailant, you must be a RAGING BULL! MAD! CRAZY! Wanting ... not just ready ... but WANTING to kill or be killed!" Doctor Bayless was shouting.

Lumchuck's eyes opened wide.

"No one fights a madman! He'll back down if you look insane!" Our instructor was walking back and forth in front of the class. His movements were jerky and he spat and frothed at the mouth when he talked.

Lumchuck raised his hand.

"Yes, Lumchuck? You trying to appear interested or intelligent?" Dr. Bayless stepped out of character and acknowledged Lumchuck's presence.

"I'm interested, Dr. Bayless." We all shook our heads in agreement with Lumchuck's honesty.

"You say we gotta look insane to our assailant?"

"Well, yes. Fear is the only edge you have."

"What if he's crazy too?" Lumchuck asked with a face so vacant only a Mother could love.

"I'll rephrase it for you Lumchuck." Dr. Bayless went into a parable.

"On July 8, 1874, the Royal Canadian Mounted Police were established in Eastern Canada, although they were then called the North-West Mounted Police. On that day 295 brave men, both Mounties and half-breeds, were given provisions, horses and paid 25 cents per day to march West. Along the way they were tasked with keeping the peace amongst the Indian tribes and the white settlers they would encounter. They were told that they had to be all those things I'm telling you to be. Sure, they were given long blue riding breeches with wide yellow stripes but they were also given a Tunic of Scarlet to wear — very similar to your Scarlet Tunic — your Red Serge. They were brave men in those days."

He paused. A calm smoothed his facial lines and the class held its collective breath. He looked out the window at the ghosts of 275 brave Scarlet Tunics riding by. In his eyes we could see the reflection. Two hundred seventy-five brave Mounties, 20 Metis drivers, 339 horses, 142 oxen and 93 head of cattle.

"The birth of a nation. Making memories and trailing dust.

"But, in truth, my dear Lumchuck," the doctor's eyes turned cold and his pupils were pinpoints of black. He leaned forward and his lower lip quivered as he spoke the words. "The truth is ... Lumchuck ... do you know why they wore that Scarlet Tunic?"

Lumchuck's fat body trembled as Doctor Bayless moved slowly closer.

"The truth is, Lumchuck, they wore Red 'cause if them brave men ever got riddled with arrows, they could bleed all day and it wouldn't show! They'd keep fighting and appear invincible! Their Scarlet Tunics would hide their blood!"

Doctor Bayless looked out over the class and his eyes turned

44

impish. "And that's why to this very day, enlisted men wear Scarlet Tunics and Commissioned Officers wear brown pants!"

The class collapsed in laughter. Except Lumchuck. He had just broken wind and still trying to regain bowel control. One hearty laugh would see him wearing the same brown trousers that officers wore.

We laughed harder.

But it wasn't a laugh which brought me back to the present. It was a single word: "PIG," followed by a beer bottle bouncing off the hood of my patrol car.

Came the voice again, "PIG!"

I slammed my foot down hard on the brakes.

"5 Brave 23 request back-up. I've got about 16 idiots. Drunk. Just been pelted with a road rocket. My 10-20 is Tolmie Drive at the Wolfe Creek Bridge."

"10-4, Two Three. Your 10-20 is Tolmie at Wolfe Creek?" Sharon confirmed my location, my 10-20.

"10-4," I answered into the microphone.

"Car to respond? Bravo Two Three needs back-up."

I heard the familiar KSSHT of a computer radio message. Someone had pushed their "Detail" button signaling they would accept the call.

"Copy Bravo Six. You're detailed. Your E.T.A.?"

"About sixty seconds." A voice answered. I recognized it.

I was lucky. Stewart Dudzinski was on his way. Half Scottish, half Polish. A wild mixture.

Four minutes ago I was wishing he would find Clarence. Now I was relieved to see his car nearly a mile away travelling on a dust comet and coming my way.

I slid the gearshift into reverse, spun gravel under the car and reversed 50 feet. Blocking the bridge was a herd of about 20 youths, all of them carrying beer. Mostly the beer was carried on the inside but a few still held onto their half-full cardboard cartons.

"Whadya got? I'm 'bout 30 seconds away!" Stu's voice came clear and calm over the radio.

"I got about 20 mutants here. Got liquor seizures galore. With any luck, enough liquor seizures to keep the Sarge happy and fill our quota for the night."

"Comin' up on you now." Stu spoke the words as his car crested the hill and slid the last 10 feet to a stop.

Stewart Dudzinski climbed out of the marked car. Although he was nearly 6½ feet tall, he weighed a mere 180 pounds. He chewed tobacco — greasy brown shredded leaves, foil wrapped with a picture of an Indian on the front. REDMAN.

Quietly he closed the driver's door of his car and smiled a lumpy smile as he walked by — on his way to becoming a legend.

"I just love these meetings." Stewart rubbed the palms of his hands together as he walked up to the youths who were already laughing at this caricature of a man.

"Hey, Pig! Is that your name tag on your shirt or you wearing an eye chart?"

Dudzinski carefully removed his blue and white name tag, placed it in his shirt pocket and fastened the button.

"Neither." His voice was soft and controlled. He walked up to the group.

"Hey, Stick-Man. Why don't you stick your tongue out. I wanna see what a walking zipper looks like!"

Stewart smiled ever-so-slightly.

"Hey, Pencil-Neck! Is that really you or am I talking to a shadow?" The wisecracks continued anonymously from the crowd of youths. We both knew this crowd. It was like all the others. Eager to lead each other, they relied on their state of alcohol-induced bravado for inner guidance.

Dudzinski walked closer, looked my way and winked. "It's show time."

I slipped away from the car and flanked the collection of drunken misfits. They moved to the edge of the bridge, not realizing they were being herded by two of the best shepherds they had ever met. Like lambs to the shearing shed they huddled together. What they could not foresee was the fact that they were being moved slowly and deliberately — not lambs, but cattle — to the slaughterhouse.

From the rear of the crowd a beer can arched over their heads towards Dudzinski. The last three feet of its travel was stopped short of its target by a large bony hand. Dudzinski's. Almost casually, the stick-man caught it and dropped the silver aluminum can at his feet.

We inched our way closer to the pack.

It was easy to see how tightly they had packed to each other. Tight, like lemmings just before their plunge from the cliff.

"Gentlemen! All we're asking is for all you fine men to leave your beer behind, turn toward home and WALK!" The calm voice of a tall, strange-looking police officer gave the command clearly and calmly. But Dudzinski meant business. I held my ground. That was easy. All the heat of this pressure cooker was about to be vented at a tall skinny cop who liked classical music, small furry animals, chewing tobacco (Redman) and one more passion in his thin, lumpy life,

KARATE!

"Please, fellas," Stewart almost pleaded. "Just drop your beer

46

and go home. I know what you're all thinking and it just won't work ... not today." Dudzinski shook his head slowly from side to side.

"You know what I'm thinking, Lumpy?" A cro-magnon cave reject emerged from the crowd. "Lumpy! I'm talking to you. Do you know what I'm thinking?" The cave-dweller arched his single eyebrow and raised an arm that was bigger than Lumpy's leg. He reached out and tapped Stewart's cheek. Dudzinski's stare didn't break. He chewed once and moved the wad of oily brown leaves to his other cheek.

"C'mon Lumpy. You gonna leave or am I gonna make you swallow? You know what I'm thinking right now?"

Dudzinski spat square in the face of the group spokesman. "I'm thinking you got one mean burn in your eyes 'bout now, son. I'm also thinking that you'd better go home while you can still walk." When Dudzinski spoke, it sounded more like fact than opinion.

An arm shot out, followed by a short burst of profanity. Dudzinski had been seized by the throat. He didn't flinch. Then he spat out one word:

"IKIO!" and grasped the thick wrist.

"NIKYO!" The thick dirty hand slid away from his throat and snapped back hard.

"SANKYO!" Both hand and arm were rotated 180 degrees and held rigid. Wrist, elbow and shoulder locked up tighter than a rusty outdoor padlock.

"KOTAGAYESHI!" A strange sound came from the caveman's arm as it rotated another 180 degrees and bent downward. The sound of a limb being torn from a tree. A brief crackle, followed by a sickening snap.

Dudzinski stepped over a body taken to the ground by the sheer weight of pain.

"Now fellas — Please?" He spat, this time on the gravel. "Please put your beer down and go home." Stu walked into the crowd. The Red Sea parted, hesitated, then went home.

"Hurt bad?" Stewart reached down, helped the quivering hulk to his feet and unceremoniously loaded him into the rear of the police car. "Mind your head, wouldn't want you to get hurt."

"I'll take this Munchkin to Emergency, get his arm plastered then book him in. I think I'll sign this cast. Never done that before. You want the beer?"

I nodded. I would get one statistic scored in my name. A "no-case seizure." Dudzinski scored twice. He would receive one point for the charges he would lay against his prisoner — assaulting a police officer. We both know it would not result in a conviction but it was a stat. The second point he would score would be for the actual arrest.

Statistics satisfied upper management and arresting a drunk, even an injured drunk, was a stat. In our personal file, a drunk was scored the same as a bank robber or rapist.

The formula was one arrest and one charge equalled two stats.

With Dudzinski went my share of the loot for the most colorful drunk. A single-eyebrowed, low-brow who could make sounds only a dog could hear would certainly qualify for the most colorful! I conceded my loss of the evening fund.

"How you gonna sign the cast?" I shouted at my friend as he telescoped back into his car.

"Batman!" He winked, spat a stream of brown liquid from his window, then drove off slowly. In the quiet he had left behind, I loaded scattered cans of beer into my trunk, pressed exhibit labels onto each one and scrawled the date and time on each tin.

Batman. I frowned at his selection. Batman was a caped crusader for justice. A broken arm was hardly justice for a few local toughs out enjoying an evening's carnage. Not hardly justice.

Briefly, I thought back to last summer. A similar incident had left me unconscious, lying on the asphalt for my buddies to find. Without a partner like Dudzinski, it was I who had been herded, clubbed from behind and left face down in the darkness of a rock-induced, dreamless sleep. I would wake up hours later, paralyzed and unable to speak for a week. I was still feeling the results of the blood clot that had lodged in my brain. It left me less prepared for life than I would ever imagine.

"I hope it hurts like Hell when they set his arm." I made a silent wish to the Pain Fairy and in my mind I could see jagged bone cutting through flesh as a doctor straightened the limb. I laughed. Damn, I hated the pukes that had forced us to be so violent. I hated the violence that we had learned to inflict first.

I hated everything.

I crawled back behind the driver's wheel and caught a glimpse of my face in the rearview mirror. I hated that, too.

COMPARTMENTALIZE!

That word had haunted me for 16 years.

Compartmentalize. To a drunk be jovial, firm and parent-like. To a grieving parent be kind, understanding and compassionate and ... to your assailant ... be a raging bull bent on total destruction.

I had only been on shift for two hours and already there were two passengers in my police car. The shadow of Clarence's parents framed the ghost of a sad, confused police officer. He sat beside me in the passenger's seat. The spirit of the raging bull was in the back seat. He was both angry and relieved. Angry because he did not have the opportunity to react like Dudzinski. Funny, though, he was relieved for the same reason. It was confusing.

Three of us. Alone. Together.

For a moment I feared the next 10 hours of a 12-hour Friday night shift. I hoped against all hope that this shift would slide by and that I would learn to forget everything I had done. For company and temporary relief, I reached deep into my briefcase and removed the Deck.

Shuffle. Cut. Flip the top card.

I read the words slowly and smiled at their magic:

> *We should never learn*
> *to forget:*
> *We can only learn by*
> *Remembering*

All my life, circumstances had molded me into becoming the man I had become. I had spent 16 years pulling dead people from twisted cars, arresting drunks who would offer their thanks in the form of a vomit pool on the floor of my police car, and knocking on doors of unsuspecting parents to inform them that their child who went swimming would be late for supper — very late.

I looked at the card again. "...we can only learn by remembering."

You really screwed up there, Corporal Withers. Many bosses had found comfort only in a bottle of whiskey. Their excuse was simple. They could not forget, so they drank to kill the pain. Remembering brought too much pain. Alcoholism, I had learned, was not a sickness, it was not weakness, it was necessary for survival. It worked for a few of them, until they retired and found out they couldn't exist on a meager government pension. They swallowed their guns in the privacy of their pain-darkened rooms.

COMPARTMENTALIZE!

That was the secret. You don't have to forget — just take each emotion, each fear and each package of pain and build a wall around them.

Like a lightening bolt, the realization came. I could be a raging bull to fight off my attacker — but that was not me. Just a part I could learn to play.

I could be a jovial parent to my next drunk, but that also was not me. Like an actor on stage, I would play that part, too.

And compassionate? Caring? Soft and kind?

What about Clarence? Could I ... would I ... merely play that part also, knowing that Smokey would follow his trail to the river. Was that only a part I would play? Like the raging bull, not really me, just an act? If I was all an act — if each part is only a temporary role I had learned to play — then who was I?

Like Alice in Wonderland, life got curiouser and curiouser. I was living in a jabberwocky world where bad guys got away, good guys lost and children died. I was afraid.

Remembering what I had learned, I quickly compartmentalized my fear, pulled my seat belt tight and leaned forward. On the way to the radio, my hand tossed the Deck into the open leather briefcase and made a dive for the familiar yellow button. "R.T.T." — Request to talk.

"KSSHT."

"5 Bravo 23 go ahead."

"Two Three's clear the Wolfe Creek Bridge. 10-18?" I was ready to take my next assignment.

I lied.

"Two Three, could you meet Echo Nine on Tact?"

"10-4." I reached over and clicked the channel selector on my radio three clicks to the right.

I keyed the mike and felt my guts twist as I called Tom. "Echo Nine, Two Three, you calling?"

"10-4 Bob, Smokey's followed ... track ... down ... water. You know anything ... paper bag?"

Tom's transmission was erratic, many words missing. Police work gave you only a few things you could depend on, with portable radios not very high on the list. They weighed 2½ pounds, wore a hole in the side of your pants and cost over $2,000. Like two of my old bosses, however, they were always guaranteed to let you down when you needed them most.

It was easy to generalize. Cynicism allowed words like "always" to replace the truth. Fatigue and cynicism had forced me to forget that my bosses — all of them — had risen through the ranks. I had forgotten that most of my superior officers were just as tired as I was. Some more so.

I replied to Tom's broken message. "Barely copy you, Tom. Go again?"

"...portable ... again. Smokey's followed ... river. I was talking to ... Henderson. You ... paper bag?"

I jigsawed the last two messages together. Tom and Smokey had followed a track down to the river's edge. He had been talking to the Hendersons and wanted to know if I had informed the parents that I had found Clarence's paper frog-bag.

I hesitated for a moment. The paper bag still under my shirt. Moist with sweat, it no longer crackled but I could feel its presence. It weighed a hundred pounds.

"You're broken, Tom. I can barely copy you. You want me to return?" I hoped he wouldn't.

"Negative. I was just ... about ... bag."

"Can't copy you, Tom. I'll check with you later."

"...-4. I'll ... down river."

I silently prayed to Saint Conundrum, patron saint of all confused cowards. I knew I would have to return to Mayberry and face the Hendersons before shift-end. But I was relieved, knowing this meeting could be postponed.

I spun the radio dial back to dispatch channel.

It was 9:00 p.m. and the sun bounced lazily along the western horizon on its way to bed. God, it was beautiful. At least there was something worth looking at tonight. I always liked sunsets. The prettier they were, the more I believed tomorrow would be a better day.

A child's poem echoed through my head. My father had taught it to me a long time ago, in a land far, far away:

"Red sky at night is a shepherds delight

Red sky in morning - sailor take warning."

Tonight, however, the sun lied. It lied to me and it lied to the Hendersons.

COMPARTMENTALIZE!

I clicked off the sympathy switch and reached for the microphone. "5 Bravo 23's back on dispatch and clear."

Metal collar badge worn on the Scarlet Tunic.

CHAPTER FOUR

THE GOOD, THE SAD AND
THE UGLY

Nothing is so strong as
True Gentleness
— or —
As gentle as True Strength.
Lao-Tse

Sunset. I envied the sun as it pulled its earthern cover over its head and went to bed. The sun never worked night shift, at least not as a cop. It always went to bed, slept well and returned the following morning; bright, clear and indifferent to man's problems.

Good night, sun. Sleep well.

Reaching down I pushed the yellow "CLR" button on my radio. I was clear ... barely. No matter how far I drove tonight, I would not be able to leave Mayberry far behind.

"10-4 Bravo 23. I've one outstanding. Clear to copy?"

I reached for my notebook, automatically like a smoker reaching for his cigarettes. The black cover flipped open to a clear page and in one movement I keyed the mike and clicked a ball point pen into action. "Go ahead."

"5 Bravo 23 we have a report of a backyard fire ... neighbor reports a lot of smoke coming from a location, one house north of her residence...."

Sharon mechanically recited the information, silently sharing with me the simple truth: Another call would only delay my return to the Hendersons.

"I repeat. One house north of 8843 Selkirk. Time dispatched is 21:10 hours. You want time in?"

"Neg." I did not need the time in — the time the call was received in the communication center. I wouldn't bother with it in my report. I knew it would only be one page long this time. I knew where I was going and who I was going to see.

21:10 hours! 9:10 p.m.! I had spent 10 minutes on the Wolfe Creek Bridge watching a sunset and trying to ignore the world around me. It would be dark in about 15 minutes and Tom would be following Smokey's glowing eyes through the brush. Smokey was unique amongst Police Dogs.

In the light of day he looked like a typical German shepherd. Healthy and muscular, with just a hint of kindness in his eyes. Flashlights and camera flashes, however, transformed him. One eye glowed red and the other reflected no light at all. Tom never allowed Smokey's photo to be taken with a flash-equipped camera. Said it made him look like a one-eyed cripple. Smokey the Cyclops.

The truth was even stranger. Smokey was wall-eyed. You never really knew which eye was looking at you. Tom knew this but wouldn't admit it except in rare circumstances when he would rout two perpetrators, stand them five feet apart and give the order. "Watch 'em Smokey. Watch 'em both."

Then Tom would stand back, thrust his hands into his gun belt and in his best Clint Eastwood voice announce: "Well, Punk, now you're wondering. Can this dog see out of both eyes or just one. You wanna run? Go ahead — MAKE MY DAY!"

No one ever took him up on his offer. Too many people had seen the movie and knew that cops never bluff. Never.

Smokey. He was my friend, too. Smokey, Tom and I were a family — fellow officers.

"KSSHHHT." The police radio alerted me of an incoming message.

"Your E.T.A. Bravo Two Three?"

I collected my thoughts and put them aside. Compartmentalized.

"I'll be there in about 10 minutes."

"10-4."

One house north of 8843 Selkirk. Jake Koraluck lived there. One mean drunken dude. Last week he torched the hedge in his front yard. When we arrived, Jake was still screaming at the evil spirits living in the bushes. Truth was, the evil spirits that had ruined his life lived in a bottle. Everyone knew that, except Jake.

Last week the front hedge, the week prior it was his cat. Paint thinner and a butane lighter. When he ignited the cat, it made a sound like a dog. WOOF! Then it died in terrible agony.

I hated that man. I hated who he was and what he had done.

I pushed down hard on the accelerator and allowed the raging bull out of his compartment. There would be no jovial parent to arrest this drunk.

The streets slid by and I lost count of the intersections as I unconsciously counted off the hundred blocks. Most policemen develop an internal guidance system. Send them on a call and their brain shifts into a three dimensional holographic map, estimating traffic flow and short cuts. They quickly find their way to any call but ask them their location along the way and they have to pause to check street signs.

Eighty-eight hundred Main Street. Hard left, four blocks and turn right. Five houses to the north I could see a black plume rising from Jake's backyard. I reached for the radio and I slowly drove to the curb and parked.

"Bravo Two Three's at scene. Request backup, please."

"10-4 Two Three. Bravo Eleven's just clearing a shoplifter at the Champlain Mall. I'll advise."

"Call Fire base too, please Sharon. We'll need some water here."

I knew there would be a fight. Jake Koraluck was 5'8" tall and weighed about 220 pounds. He loved to fight when he was drunk. He had loved to fight every time I had met him. Tonight, I swore — he'd sober up.

I waited curbside for Bravo Eleven. I would need cover on this call. Jake would be drunk, that was a given. I knew I could drop kick him half way into his next life but once he was on the deck, I'd need help loading him into the back of my patrol car.

The smoke was getting thick but there was no structure involved. Just smoke. Thick black smoke. It smelled like burning rubber.

"Well, I've two or three minutes to kill, Corporal Withers, what can you tell me 'bout this call?" I spoke the words out loud. I often talked to myself — the company wasn't much, but it was all I had. Reaching over to my right, I dipped into my briefcase and retrieved the Deck from its resting place.

Shuffle, cut, turn over top card:

> *The injuries we inflict*
> *and the injuries we see —*
> *Are always measured on*
> *different scales.*

The card fit. After seeing a cat curl up and sputter like a piece of bacon on a hot griddle, I was about to inflict some serious injury on fat Jake. Sixteen years of experience had taught me how to inflict injuries that could never be seen. Never measured.

Time for one more card:

> *It's what you learn —*
> *after you "know-it-all" —*
> *that really matters.*

I already knew that — and it didn't matter.

There was only one thing that mattered. Koraluck. For the past two years he had been a thorn in our collective side. Besides burning bushes and cats, he had beaten his wife and had lived off welfare cheques. Without them he could never have afforded his booze.

"Why shouldn't I drink? The government buys it for me!" That was Jake's only excuse and it could not be argued that, indeed, his chronic alcoholic haze was government sponsored.

Headlights in my rearview mirror. Bev pulled in behind me, turned off her lights and killed the engine. I sat and waited while she radioed in her 10-7 and popped out of her car. Bev always popped. All 5'4" inches of her. She was like a breath of fresh air, always cheery, always eager and always ready to help.

Unfortunately, Bev was a woman. Female police officers were not well liked. Most supervisors openly admitted their disgust at having to work with a crip — short for cripple. Any police officer could easily establish his manhood by referring to his female counterpart as an emotional, intellectual or physical cripple. But Bev was different. She had been baptized by fire the night she lost a fight to William Curtis — also known as "Wiener."

Wiener was the Sergeant-at-Arms of our local Hell's Angels Chapter. No one knows how or why he was named Wiener, only that it referred to a courageous act he had performed during his initiation into the club. Courageous by biker standards, sick and disgusting by any sane human.

Bev was a beautiful girl but one of the "cripples." The night she stood up to Wiener, however, we learned the truth — we were all equal.

Wiener was a graduate of three Kick Boxing Championships and had sent two of our officers to early pension. His goal in life was to be shot by a Mountie. Our goal was to help him achieve his goal. We all prayed for the day Wiener would pull a knife on a police officer.

In advance, our watch agreed on the inscription we would place on his headstone:

"Here lies Wiener,
Not too bright.
He brought his knife
To a cop gunfight."

Wiener had beaten every cop he fought.

But not Bev. She was different. Bev knew the rules and in a back alley one warm summer evening she took him on. Bev lost — sort of. Her injuries healed in less than a month but when the paramedics forced an airway down her almost lifeless throat they found, inside her mouth, half chewed, Wiener's ear!

After Bev had recovered from her injuries, she placed her trophy-ear in a jar of tequila. At every party when male bonding was in full swing and our self-told stories of heroism became ever-so-slightly inflated, out came the Wiener-jar with a soft "pour you a drink,

Officer? It really doesn't taste bad. I've tried it!"

No one. No one had ever taken Bev up on her offer to drink from her Wiener-jar, but in each soft offer she had reminded us men that we could never establish a monopoly on bravery.

Bev was a Police Officer who had worked her way into our fraternity and our hearts. Bev, like Tom and Smokey, was special to me. Friends.

"Hey, Bobo, you gonna sit there or get out and work with us women?"

No one called me Bobo except for Bev and one other. I looked out from my car. Bev was smiling and slapping the palm of her left hand with a black steel flashlight she carried. She never carried a baton, sap or night-stick. Instead, a black steel, five-cell flashlight called Leroy followed her everywhere. Often Bev would face up to an opponent and tell him fairly, "See this? I calls him Leroy! He's my buddy! He shines through the darkness and helps me through the long lonely nights."

Just as her enemy made a rude comment or aggressive move, Leroy would arc forward and break his collar bone. You can't fight with a smashed collar bone. Can't even raise your arm. It was a trick Bev had learned shortly after her midnight meet with Wiener and with that trick came a vow to take Wiener's other ear.

"C'mon, Bobo, we collar Jake and I'll split the prize for the biggest!"

Bev had never won the Friday night drunk fund. Once she almost scooped her share by arresting a hermaphrodite. "Half-man, half-woman, which cell-block do we put this one in?" Those words still echoed faintly off the hard cell walls. She was smiling when she booked in her prize but through her grin you could see guilt and shame for having entered such a sick contest.

Even that arrest, however, was overshadowed by the arrival of E.T.

E.T. was a mistake of nature who had been forced into the mold of "drunk" through constant pain and humiliation. He was shorter than Bev by at least five inches. One night after a pitiful attempt at assaulting an officer, he had to be choked out. As he lay there on the cold cement floor of the cell block, it was noticed how he resembled a Smurf. E.T. had large bulbous eyes that barely closed, even when he slept. His toes on both feet were joined together and shared one common toenail. E.T., our captive extra-terrestrial, had no thumbs.

After the first night that nature's mistake had spent in the drunk tank, he no longer qualified for the "most colorful drunk" prize. E.T. was revolting and pitiful. Revolting because he reminded us of just how cruel we could be and pitiful because nature had let him live such a painful life. We all knew why he drank. Hell, we drank to kill the pain that life gave us, too!

Each weekend, E.T. would find a home in our cells. He was the only drunk that ever rated a blanket and pillow. He was the only drunk who rated our friendship and understanding. Then one Friday night in the middle of winter, E.T. snuggled down in his favorite cell and finally closed his eyes — forever.

I took the small one-inch plastic name tag from his cell door that night as they carried his poor body away. I didn't even say goodbye.

"C'mon, Bobo!" Leroy was tapping at the window.

"Sorry, Bev." I opened the door and climbed out. "I was...."

"Daydreaming again?"

"Ya."

"Keep that up and Schlitz is gonna tack your ears to the bulletin board!"

I slammed the door hard.

"KSSHHHT, Two Three." I adjusted the squelch on my portable radio, removed it from the belt clip and answered. "Bravo Two Three."

"Fire Base notified and enroute your point with a pumper. They say five minutes. 10-4?"

"10-4. Thanks, Sharon."

I clipped the radio back on my belt and walked across the street to Jake's house. Bev was three steps ahead of me, as usual.

The gravel covering Jake's driveway crunched under our feet and my thoughts drifted back to Mayberry. But Bev kept me anchored in the here and now.

"Heads up, Dreamer. Last week Jake was playing frisbee with a hub cap. Wonder what he'll throw at us tonight?"

We rounded the corner of the house and stood in the darkness, quietly laughing yet saddened by what we saw.

Jake was sitting on an overturned galvanized steel bucket. Unceremoniously, he had skewered three ball-park franks on a coat hanger and was enjoying his own private backyard barbecue.

His barbecue was unique. Two old rubber tires smoked and reluctantly gave off a dirty orange flame. Beside the fire, a one-gallon gas can, nearly empty, had served as Jake's barbecue starter fluid.

Jake was singing the Alcoholic's National Anthem in 2/4 time. Sung à la self-pity:

"Nobody know the trouble I've seen

Nobody knows my sorrow.

Nobody knows the trouble I've seen...."

BELCH!

"I don't believe it. This is precious." Bev's face lit up when she realized that Jake was a contender for the biggest and most colorful drunk prize.

We slowly walked up behind the fat man and watched for a few seconds more. He was alone in his own world. Just like us.

"Nobody knows the trouble I've seen...."

Bev reached out and placed her hand on Jake's left shoulder. His round body rotated on the bucket.

"Glory hallelujah!" he finished his song.

"Your wieners are on fire." Bev motioned to the black, fat-dripping wieners on the end of the wire.

"You'd be burning too if I stuck you in the fire!" Jake winked. In his twisted, numb mind he thought he was being funny. The black burnt wiener residue which encircled his mouth, however, was a sign of sickness, not humor.

"Jake, just look at yourself. You got more burnt weenie on your face than in your mouth!"

"Yes, Mother." Jake ridiculed the parent/child communication that Bev was attempting. He turned back to the fire to thrust his tube steak shisk kebob back into the dirty inferno. Jake pretended we were no longer there. Like most alcoholics, denial was his only coping tool. Ignore the problem and it does not exist!

"C'mon, Jake, let's go." Bev once again placed her hand on his shoulder.

"I'm on private property. You got no grounds to arrest me. A man's home is his castle!"

Jake was telling the truth. We had no authority to arrest a drunk on his own property. Yet somehow he had to be removed. It was our sworn duty "to protect, to serve and to put out all Good Year Barbecues" so the public could rest safe in their home. A wimpy municipal by-law threatened a $15 fine if Jake did not put out the blaze, but his next welfare cheque was only a few days away and he could afford that. Somehow, a ticket for "illegal trash burning" did not seem to fit this occasion.

We had to put out the fire. The neighbors wanted clean air. They would not accept any excuse from us, yet if we took action on private property, ol' Schlitz would get all chubby inside as he raked us over his own set of coals. Jake would get a free lawyer from Legal-Aid, sue us both and our jobs would be toast. False arrest was a charge I had already faced. That was the day I learned the simple facts. A child molester had more rights than a Police Officer. I did not want to go down that road again. The R.C.M.P. bought me a lawyer but I had to work my own way out of the ulcers it had left me with.

"A man's home is his castle!" Jake repeated.

Bev walked slowly away from the fire. "Well, I'd better tell Doris she can't cross your moat."

"Doris?" Jake stood up, steadied himself and looked at Bev's form disappearing into the darkness.

"If that Bitch is here I'll kill her!"

Jake half-ran, half-stumbled away from the fire. In one hand he held a near-empty bottle of Jack Daniels; in the other, a wire coat hanger with two charred wieners. One had just dropped into the fire.

I followed close behind Jake as he mumbled something about falling from a ladder that his wife, Doris, should have been holding onto. They had been married for over 20 years and for some unknown reason, within a period of only a few weeks, Doris had left him. Jake moved his place of residence to the interior of a whiskey bottle and became a very bitter half-man. Maybe he had fallen on his head.

"God Damned leg has never been the same. I'll kill the Bitch!" Jake was limp-stumbling faster and faster, following Bev up his driveway and out onto the street.

It was a ploy that worked often. If you can't arrest a drunk on private property, find a way to lure him out onto the street. It worked with anyone whose brain was numbed beyond normal thinking.

Jake walked out onto the center of the street and wobbled like a slow spinning top as he looked in all directions for his wife. Bev had taken up post on the sidewalk and was smiling. She had already won!

"Gotcha, Jake. You're in a public place now and you're under arrest for being drunk!"

Jake had been had. "I'm goin' back in, around, over or through you." Jake hurled his skewer at her but held on tight to his bottle.

"It'll have to be through me." Bev matched his moves, shifting her position from side to side.

"I've been shafted by one woman already and you ain't big enough to make it two!"

"Back off, Jack." Bev held her position as Leroy rose to the occasion.

"Outa' my way Bitch!" Jake was drunk but he was quick. A ham-sized fist slammed into Bev's chest, launching her backwards into a half-dead hedge.

"Jake! Whoa!" I held both my hands out in front.

"You gonna let me by or we gonna dance, too?" Jake was too big to dance with so I stepped aside.

"Call me Bitch?" Bev had crawled to her feet and was only an arm's length from her assailant. She faced him head-on. "Last guy that called me bitch got to be a land owner!"

Jake dropped his guard for a split second. Facing Bev square on, he looked confused. "Land owner?"

"Ya. I gave him two achers!" Bev's right leg swung out like an uncoiled spring and found its home neatly in Jake's crotch.

THUK!

Time stood still.

Jake did not even flinch. Something was happening that neither Bev nor I understood. Most men would have been hopelessly paralyzed, lying in a pool of their own vomit.

But ol' Jake just stood there. Still and quiet. He looked deep into Bev's eyes and spoke slowly. "You're the second woman to hurt me there." Jake sucked in the cool night air. "And you're gonna be the last!"

Jack Daniels fell to the ground and smashed into a hundred spiritual pieces. Jake didn't even look down. Slowly he walked across the macadam towards Bev. Matching his speed, I intersected his path. He did not even acknowledge my presence. He could not. Like a hawk in a power dive, he saw only one object and he was headed for it. Bev.

I slowed to allow Jake to walk by and quickly slid my left arm under his chin as I stepped into position behind him. With Jake's chin resting in the crook of my left elbow, I brought my hand across the right side of his neck and gripped my right bicep. His neck was now locked in place and the snare was complete. With my right hand I pushed the back of his head forward.

CAROTID CONTROL!

I held firmly. He could breath and was in no pain so he did not even struggle. This type of police hold was painless, humane and effective. It only restrained; that is, for the first 12 seconds. Then it worked its magic.

Twelve seconds. Twelve seconds is a very long time when you are riding the back of a 250-pound drunk. In 12 seconds you can call for help, squirm into a better position, tighten the hold or as I did ...

REMEMBER.

Corporal Franz Leitz was our self-defense instructor at the Police Academy. Lean, muscular and sadistic, Leitz insisted his first name was Fritz. Said it meant "slow-death" in some obscure language. Fritz was well suited for the job. Our first day in his class began when he lined us all against the cement wall and proudly declared:

"If I had my way I would shoot you all in the heart and get it over with. Instead, I've been given the privilege of pulverizing, bruising and taking you all apart limb-from-limb, piece-by-piece in the next six months."

He had our attention.

"My name is Corporal Fritz Leitz. I am 5'11" tall. I weigh 178 pounds and I come from pure stock. I can see by looking at you mixed

60

pack of half-breeds that none of you will ever be my physical or mental match. So I'll just do the best I can with each one of you genetic mutants."

Corporal Leitz often called us half-breeds, even if we weren't. He would point to his close-cropped blond hair and remind us that his parents were not part anything — they were pure and so was he. Every time he addressed us singly, he would prefix any comment he had by asking us what kind of animal our Mother had sex with nine months before we were born. Humiliation was supposed to be a toughening procedure but it did little to make us better men.

Everyone feared this man. He was near-crazy. In the first few months one of our troop-mates who was a Mormon declared he had traced Leitz's genealogy back to the Nazi death camp of Auschwitz. When confronted with this, Corporal Leitz smiled.

We did not.

It was our first self-defense lesson with Fritz Leitz and he was about to establish a pecking order, placing himself at the top.

"I want to show you all what a fourth degree Black Belt can do. Lumchuck, take one step forward. Now!"

Lumchuck stepped forward and snapped to attention.

"Thank you for volunteering. Walk toward me."

As our fat friend waddled into Leitz's body space, the Auschwitz descendant slammed Norman's right shoulder back hard, spinning him around and letting him fall backwards into Leitz's sadistic trap. Our Arian Master threw his left arm around Lumchuck's neck and locked it into place.

"This is CAROTID CONTROL!

"As I hold this fat pig in my grip, I will compress his sterno-cledo mastoid muscles against his carotid arteries. I am now restricting the blood flow to his brain. But you can't feel any difference can you, Lumchuck?"

Norman did not respond. He was too frightened.

"Now resist, Jew-boy." Leitz spoke quietly into Lumchuck's ear but a couple of us in the front row could hear and understand what was happening. "Go ahead. Resist. Escape if you can."

Suddenly this was not funny. Norman tried to escape but he could not.

"Watch his eyes! Nine, 10, 11, 12, 13 — they should be rolling up inside his head by now."

Lumchuck's eyes obeyed the command and rolled upwards, exposing only the white portion of his eyes. He stiffened for a second, shuddered then went limp.

"Now to complete this, I just hang him for a few more seconds...."

Our friend's body hung, by the neck. He was twitching all over. "...then I release."

None of us will ever forget the sickening sound that Norman's head made that day when he was dropped backwards onto the tile floor. Like a ripe melon struck with a wood club. Hard but hollow.

We all watched in horror as Lumchuck's body lay on the floor, twitching and convulsing in an anoxia-induced seizure.

"Don't worry, he's asleep now and can't feel a thing. Won't even have a sore head when he wakes up."

Lumchuck was regaining consciousness. Glassy-eyed, he slowly managed to sit up, then stand and walk back to his place in the troop. Mysteriously, he rubbed the back of his head and frowned. He did not know it wasn't supposed to hurt.

Corporal Leitz shouted. "This is carotid control and all you have to do is compress the carotid artery. This artery carries blood to the brain and your victim, without any blood in his brain, goes down! Carotid control!" he yelled. "Give me the carotid and I can control the world!" Corporal Leitz was clearly insane. He had a fourth degree Black Belt, but not in Karate. Leitz had studied sadism and we feared for our survival.

"Constable Bryant, c'mere. You're next."

Andre Bryant was a tall, lanky recruit whose complexion had barely left puberty. Andre never said much, and he kept to himself most of the time, yet he was liked by everyone in the troop. He possessed a quiet confidence that made him somehow superior, yet likable.

"Give me the carotid and I'll control the world!"

Leitz re-affirmed our fear.

"Bryant, walk towards me and I'll show you my own version of the Japanese choke-hold."

Andre, the gentle giant, calmly entered Leitz's forbidden body space and was instantly seized by the windpipe.

The consequence was startling. In one smooth motion, Andre raised his right arm and sunk his forefinger, knuckle deep, into the side of Corporal Leitz's neck. What happened next became a legend, only to be whispered late at night, after lights-out.

Leitz fell to the ground. Straight and hard. It was as though Andre had somehow mastered Mr. Spock's Vulcan Nerve Pinch and was teaching it to a classroom full of Trekkies.

After two or three seconds, Andre retrieved his finger from inside the neck of a near-lifeless body. He stood straight and faced us. The student had become the teacher. "The world does not need to be controlled by the likes of this man."

He looked down at the defeated Shell. "This one will wake up shortly. Just two or three ounces of pressure on two very important nerves and you can paralyze the heart and diaphragm. No heart beat, no breathing, no one to control the world. It's better this way."

Andre took his place in the troop beside Lumchuck.

"You O.K., Lumpy?" Andre was the only person who called him Lumpy without insulting him.

Norman Lumchuck shook his head. A few of us heard a faint "Thanks, buddy."

We would later learn that Constable Andre Bryant was a 28-year-old Master of Rewkaido, an art so obscure it was unknown to all but the most advanced practitioners of the martial arts.

Corporal Leitz stirred, opened his eyes and stood up slowly. He mumbled something about not feeling very well and dismissed the class. He would remember nothing of the incident but he would never again be brutal to anyone in our troop.

As we filed out of the gymnasium, Bryant smiled, we laughed and Fritz ... well he just left.

"BOB! LET HIM GO! HE'S OUT!"

Bev pulled me back quickly from the past and I could feel the weight of a 250-pound unconscious drunk pulling me down. Carefully, I guided Fat Jake's dirty face to the ground and laid it softly to rest.

"Jeeezuz! I thought you were never going to release him. He'll sleep for a month."

In my reverie I had hung poor Jake for an extra 10 seconds. That was unfortunate. With no oxygen going to the brain, all of Jake's muscles had relaxed. Totally!

Jake had filled his pants, front and back. Poor Jake.

Wretching from the smell, we rolled him over and managed to fit the handcuffs over his wrists without touching his pants. When he woke up, we helped him into the back seat of a police car.

"We'll use yours." Bev nodded in the direction of my unit. "You made the mess. You deal with it."

Bev stayed behind and waited for the Fire Department as I drove Jake back to the cells. I rolled the window down, turned the fan on and hung a green pine-tree deodorant around Jake's neck for the journey back.

The ride back to the police station was quiet. For some strange reason, there was no string of profanity coming from this drunk. We even managed to talk for a while. The voice in the back seat told me a broken, disjointed story of his wife leaving him because he'd been sick.

"C'mon, Jake, your wife left you because you spent a couple of weeks in the hospital? Problem with you is that you can't face up to the truth. You got no guts Jake. No balls at all."

"Ya." Jake agreed with me for the first time.

Twenty minutes later, the papers were filled out and I was turning the key on Jake's cell door. "Tell me, Jake. How come that lady-cop couldn't take you out with one kick? You wearin' hardware?"

"You said it earlier." Jake looked down at the floor. "I got no balls."

I laughed. His joke wasn't that funny, but I laughed. As I turned to leave, faintly from the other side of an iron-barred door I heard one word "...cancer."

I had nothing in common with Jake but I managed to share the same coping strategy he used when the truth became unbearable. Denial. I denied hearing his last words. Life was easier that way.

"Coffee's on." Walt, our night-shift guard, always kept the coffee hot and strong. After booking in a drunk, there was a ritual cleansing to be performed. A quick wash and a slow coffee.

I washed my hands in the green liquid disinfectant soap marked "For Hospital Use Only - Not For Resale" and enjoyed the hot water as it washed away all I had done and everything I had touched.

"Coffee?" Walt was pouring two cups. He knew the answer.

"No sugar, Walt, just dose it up with some of that white chemical stuff."

Walt poured whitener on the top of the coffee and stirred it in. The kitchen was situated about 10 feet from the drunk tank. It was small, dark and it smelled like fresh coffee and stale puke. A small white table and two chairs furnished the room that had heard a thousand stories and confessions.

I sipped my coffee quietly, trying not to burn my upper lip. Walter played a game with his, tipping his cup from side to side, seeing how far he could manage to slope it without spilling any of the brown liquid.

"Jake bugs you doesn't he." Walter's British/Lancashire accent was thick.

"Ya."

"It's a shame, you know — I guess Fate sort of threw him up against a pretty hard wall."

"I don't want to hear it!" I was still practising denial as a psychic soother and Walt was interfering.

Walter was a magic sort of fellow. Always told you what you needed to hear when you needed to hear it most. He was short, 62 years old and built from flesh and steel. His thick arms bore an assortment of tattoos he had collected from "The War To End All Wars," but no matter what he wore, his heart always shone through.

"Nope — not tonight. Don't want to hear it." I looked at my

coffee, hoping Walt would change his line of questioning.

"Still got that fancy deck of yours?"

I look up at Walt and smiled. "Yes. Why?"

"Go get it and we'll let it decide whether or not you want to know 'bout old Jake."

A few minutes later I was cutting the Deck.

"Top card." Walt reached out and directed the turning of the card. He was one of the few friends I had ever shared the Deck with. I did not want too many people in my world — it got too crowded once and I swore never again. But Walter was special.

I turned over the top card.

The best way to get out
of difficulty is —
To go through it.

"Okay, Walter, load and lock. Tell me about old Jake." I gave in to the Deck and Walter's wishes. It was two against one and I learned at an early age never to pick a fight when the odds were against you.

"Not much to tell, really." A drop of coffee slid down the outside of his cup. "I was just seeing if you had the guts to know your enemy. In the war, we never knew our enemy 'cept by a few dirty names we called them. Killing was easier then ... but if you ever got to know your enemy, he seemed to change somehow. Into a friend, a prisoner maybe, but no longer an enemy."

"And Jake?" I asked.

"Jake went in the hospital and came out less of a man than he could stand. Cancer of the testicles. The kind you don't ever want."

"And his wife? His drinking? The cat?" Divorce and alcoholism were misfortunes I could understand. Nearly one third of the members on my watch were either one or the other. But torching an innocent cat?

"Jake's wife left him for another man three days after he got out of the hospital. The bottle sort of took her place. Numbs his pain, I suppose. Hell, you know that."

"The cat? Jynx I think he called him."

"That cat could do something that Jake could never do again. Every time he saw that animal on the prowl, he felt less of a man. Finally, one day too much booze and the cat started talking to him — called him by name and he thought the Devil had arrived earlier than planned. Jake was trying to kill the Devil. He's cried himself to sleep many times since ol' Jynx fried."

"Earlier than planned?" I wondered about Walter's choice of words.

"Jake has only a couple of months left. The cancer's spreading upwards through his body. Says he's got a couple bottles of morphine syrup in the house but booze works as well and tastes better. Truth of the matter is that he wasn't drunk when he lit poor Jynx on fire. It was the morphine. Kinda makes some people hallucinate, I've heard."

Finally, I knew the enemy and he ceased to exist. I felt ashamed.

"May I?" A row of tattoos reached out for the Deck.

"Okay — go ahead and try them" Walt liked playing the Deck once in a while and he knew this was a special favor I allowed only the closest of friends to indulge in.

"I always ask this deck of yours a question first." His accent grew thicker. "Deck, listen up ... I'm talking to you now. My friend here is bloody depressed ... got a right to be ... so what next?"

Shuffle, cut, turn over top card:

> *You cannot do a kindness*
> *too soon because —*
> *You never know how soon,*
> *it will be too late.*

Walter and I looked calmly at each other. The silence in the room grew deafening.

"Well?" Walt's thick eyebrows raised as he asked me a world of questions in a single word.

"I once heard that we view the world through a rear-view mirror. I guess that's why we walk backwards into the future."

"Words!" Walt wiped the rim of his coffee cup with his forefinger and licked it. He looked back at me as I wrapped the cards and nested them in the breast pocket of my nylon patrol jacket.

"It's about time I started walking forward." I left Walt sitting alone in the kitchen, took in a deep breath of stale air and walked down the cement corridor to Jake's cell. For a moment I stopped, not knowing why, a twinge of cowardice I suppose. Then I turned left and walked the distance to Jake's cubicle.

Most drunks were fast asleep five minutes after booking in. Tonight, something was different. Jake had washed himself in the tiny porcelain sink and looked almost sober.

"Jake?" I called, as a tired pair of eyes looked up.

"Yes?"

That was the night I lost an enemy. Thoughts, feelings and words were spoken between two very lonely men. Words too sacred ever to be repeated.

As our hatred for each other died, something else was born. Friendship. Through the iron bars, a handshake sealed this friendship. I came to know Jake as a human being. Confused, in pain and sad — but a human being.

Just before we parted company that night, I found myself absent-mindedly peeling away remnants of some old sticky tape from Jake's cell door. Sticky tape that once held a sign which read: "E.T. SLEPT HERE."

Rest in Peace, E.T.

Cloth shoulder patch worn on uniform.

CHAPTER FIVE

DIRTY, FILTHY, SCUM-DOGS

No one knows the age of the
Human Race, but we all agree:
That it is old enough
to know better.

After learning the truth about the unfortunate Jake Koraluck, I left the office the same way I came in, through the prisoner-entrance door. Feeling better than I had in a long time, I climbed into my police car and drove out of the parking lot.

As I pulled up to a stop sign, I reached down and thumbed the CLR yellow button on my radio.

"10-4 Bravo Twenty Three, you're clear. Heard anything from Echo Six?"

"Negative, I've been in the cells."

"10-4. You going to drop out to the Henderson's? You're clear to do so."

"Neg. I'll wait 'till I hear from Tom."

"10-4. I have you back on the screen. No calls stacked."

I looked at my watch. It was midnight. Tom would have had enough time to track Clarence half-way to Hell. The river bank was a lot closer, yet no word. What was going on?

Midnight. The witching hour. In another hour, the beer parlors would be letting out and we'd be busy seeing how many drunks we could stack inside our prisoner van. A van designed to transport six people had set new limits in human endurance its first night out. We all laughed when upper management purchased a six-passenger step van. I had never heard of a Friday night with less than 20 drunks.

Six passengers!

The first night in use, it set a record when it brought back 10 prisoners. Greasy, smelly and oily, like sardines in a tin — 10 prisoners in a six-passenger bun wagon.

Every Friday night since then, a challenge existed. See how many drunks you can fit in the wagon. Three months after the purchase of the prisoner van our watch set a record which was never challenged.

Twenty-three! Twenty three bits of human flesh packed for transport to the Handcuff Hilton. The last six detainees, however, were midgets from a Halloween party. Each one dressed in a furry coat pretended to be an Ewok destined to save the life of Luke Skywalker, legendary hero of the Star Wars trilogy.

Unfortunately, because they were midgets, all other watches accused us of cheating.

"Contest rules say all prisoners must be adults." Staff Sergeant Hall passed out the rules to all watches when she heard we had beaten her watch by five. Later that week, a vote was held and midgets were declared "Official Adults." We had won the prize which had been growing slowly with a $5 donation from each weekend night shift.

The whole situation was quite embarrassing. Booking in six of God's Little People presented its own problems. We found them hiding under the benches in the back of the van like tiny mice in a vivisection lab and had to hook their tiny bodies out with a broom. At the booking-in counter we didn't have to remove their handcuffs, they fell off. Everyone had to be hoisted up to sign for their effects and we all knew there would be complaints of harassment the following day. Still, it was worth it.

The only harassment we could document was against Officer Burton, who arrived at the site of the noisy party complaint. A beer bottle thrown by one of the little darlings had careened off his shin, opening up a cut that would take 14 stitches to close. It didn't hurt that much though. Buffy Burton would later give evidence in court that the second beer bottle hit him in the face and knocked him out cold. Shame — he was never the same after that. Always drank beer from a styrofoam cup.

Z-W-I-I-I-Z

Damn, I hate it when someone interrupts my day dreaming. A car had just zwiiized through the intersection. It was definitely zwiiizing over the speed limit.

I turned right, pushed down hard on the accelerator and reached for the mike. "Bravo Two Three in pursuit of British Columbia Plates — Sierra Juliet Tango, six-seven-five, northbound on One Seventy-six Street from Nicholson Road.

"Copy Two Three. Car to cover?"

Silence.

Sharon had no cars in reserve. Every member of the watch was either on a call or out of their car trying to reach their nightly quota of liquor seizures, park patrols or impaired drivers. I was on my own.

"No problem, Sharon. I'll advise." I closed the distance and tried to pace the black Trans Am. Most judges wanted at least one-quarter mile pace before they would consider a speeding conviction.

"Bravo Two Three, that plate comes back on a 1987 Trans Am, black. Want the registered owner?"

"Neg. Hang onto the printout for me please, Sharon, he's pulling over already. I'll be out at the bottom of Stinky Barn Hill."

"10-4. I'll put you on a timer."

Sharon punched a few keys on her computer. Taking care of 20 cars was no small task. When you were put on a timer, it meant an alarm would sound on her console and our car number would blink on her screen if you did not key your mike within five minutes. Keying your mike cancelled the timer.

We were both pulled over onto the pea-gravel shoulder and I turned on my high beams. The extra light would help illuminate the Trans Am and blind the driver when he looked back in my direction. Most other police departments equipped their cars with high intensity take-down lights for this purpose. Our Force, however, thought the additional $50 expense on a police car was extravagant. A few years prior, I lost a friend to an assailant's bullet only a mile from Stinky Barn Hill. We had often complained that an ounce of extravagance would be worth a pound of remorse, but management knew better.

I approached the car on foot. Walking slowly, I held my flashlight away from my body and shone it directly into the driver's window. In my mind a lesson from the Academy still echoed: "Shoot at the light and you'll only hit my left hand. That still leaves my gun-hand free!" It was a good, safe technique but it looked silly when viewed from a neutral position.

"Good evening Sir ... uh ... ma'am. Do you realize how fast your were going?" I asked a wonderful question. I knew the car was speeding, doing at least 20 miles per hour over the speed limit, but I could not close the gap quick enough to maintain an accurate quarter-mile pace. If she said she was not sure of her speed or did not even know how fast she was travelling, I would jot down her words. In court she would face a conviction.

The judge would be compelled to look her straight in the eye and declare: "How can you tell me today that you were not speeding when you told the officer you did not even know how fast you were going?"

It was a good question that worked well for speeders. If they admitted to knowing their speed, a confession of just two or three miles per hour over the speed limit would be offered in most cases. Either way, their own words would convict them. Although we rarely charged a driver who was exceeding the limit by less than eight miles per hour, an admission in court of even one mile per hour resulted in a mandatory conviction.

It was a crazy law, but we knew how to work it. Once caught in the trap, speeders rarely escaped. Rarely.

"Huh?"

"Do you realize just how fast you were going?" I repeated.

"Yes, Officer, I was speeding."

I was not ready for an honest answer

"Oh," I answered. The lady was in her mid-thirties, casually dressed and sweating heavily. Something was wrong.

"You okay, Ma'am?" I asked, fanning my flashlight through the interior of her car, looking for anything suspicious.

She blushed, gripped the steering wheel hard and stuttered: "Officer, if I don't get to the bathroom real soon I'm gonna explode. I gotta go BAD! Please keep my license, keep my purse, keep everything! I'll pick it all up later. Please let me go!" She was pleading.

There are few excuses honest or sincere enough to elicit the sympathy of a Police Officer. This, however, was one of them. It was easy to identify with this situation. I had been in it. Police work was one of the few professions where eating, drinking and going to the bathroom were optional pleasures.

"Go!" I pointed down the road.

"Pardon?"

"Where do you live?"

"Four blocks up and turn right. Small white house on the left."

"Get outa here — GO — I understand!"

"God, thanks. Thanks. Thanks."

She tore up the gravel as her black car accelerated into the darkness, leaving behind a quickly fading set of tail-lights. I had done my good deed for the night. Saved a damsel in distress ... or at very least a lady with a weak bladder. It felt good. But not for long.

Back behind the wheel I keyed the mike.

"Two Three 10-8."

"Two Three received. Your license comes back on a late model Trans Am registered to Teresa Friedman. Don't suppose she pulled the weak bladder move on you, did she? Our query log shows it worked three times so far this month."

Silence.

"Bravo-Twenty-Three?" Sharon called.

"Neg. Sharon. She tried it but it didn't work this time." I lied. Lying was permissible when it prevented a Police Officer from being sucker punched by a woman. Police Officers are a brave lot. They are trained to valiantly face bullets, bikers and rescue children from burning houses. Their own vulnerability, however, is not high on the list of things to be conquered.

I'd been had. I felt dirty, small and weak. Most of all I felt vulnerable. It was a bad feeling.

"Bravo Twenty-Three, clear for a call?"

I raised the mike to my lips.

"10-4, Sharon. Whatdya got."

"Mrs. Williston just called the office demanding an officer attend her house tonight. She is very upset about a break-in last month. States you are the investigator.

I remembered the call.

"Two Three received. I have her address in my notebook. No need to generate a second file, I'll add any additional information onto the original report."

"She's still on the line. What's your E.T.A.?"

"Advise her I'll be about ten minutes."

"10-4."

Mrs. Williston was a retired elementary school teacher. She wore her white hair in a tight bun and represented everything a young body feared.

Margaret Williston lived deep inside the memory of every adult male. As I recalled our meeting, feelings returned ... feelings I hadn't had since the day I got my knuckles rapped for chewing gum in class. Margaret Williston made me feel nervous. She represented everything disciplined, neat and orderly that had ever been forced into a young mind. Even the throw cushions in her house sat at attention.

I had followed Mrs. Williston from room to room as she described with detail every item that had been moved by the perverts who broke into her house. Pointing out open cupboard doors and other pieces of evidence she had catalogued, she still held tight onto her wooden ruler, carefully instructing me how to investigate this crime. It was the same ruler my teacher had used. I think she inherited it.

I swallowed the gum I was chewing. And rubbed my knuckles.

I thumbed back 20 or so pages in my notebook and read that I had attended her house three weeks ago. Someone had entered through an open bathroom window while she was out doing whatever retired school teachers do. Nothing had been taken except a few dollars loose change and a part-bottle of lemon gin she kept for medicinal purposes. The thieves had overlooked her prized collection of plastic jewelry and strong perfume. For a refreshing change they had not even gone on a rampage inside her house. No damage. A few throw cushions had assumed a more relaxed position on the sofa, but there was no damage.

I turned left onto Wiltshire Boulevard, drove eight blocks then turned right. This was an area of town well suited for old retired school teachers. Every house had a white picket fence and a dainty flower bed. The street sign read Eyremont Crescent, but it might just as well have read Spinster Street.

Pulling into Margaret Williston's driveway, I radioed in my 10-7 and jotted the time in my notebook. It was an hour past midnight. What was Mrs. Williston doing awake at this ungodly hour? Except for the usual "Adults-Only" entertainment on the pay-channel, even television offered little amusement at this hour. Mrs. Williston would never bring herself to view any movies which warned "Occasional Nudity and Suggestive Language." Never.

The brick stairs in front of the house were worn and grooved with age. I walked up to the door, paused for a second, then knocked. The door opened quickly. I was expected.

"Evening, Mrs. Williston. I just received a call that you wanted to see me. It's horribly late, is there a problem?"

Margaret Williston had more color in her face than I had ever seen in a retired school teacher before. She was flushed. Was she angry, frightened or embarrassed? Her television was turned off.

I entered the house. I wasn't invited — I was ordered. As I walked by her television, I casually looked down and noticed the pay-channel guide. It lay open on top of her set. Today's date. Neatly underlined was the time, 11:30 p.m. and the title: "Cannibal Women in the Avocado Jungle of Death."

I smiled and popped a fresh stick of gum in my mouth. Juicy Fruit!

"I've been meaning to call the Police Station all day, young man. At first I thought no, I should not do this but I finally convinced myself that you should know what horrible people you have out there!" A knobby finger fanned the direction where the horrible people could be found.

"I really do not mean to bother you officer, but I have finally decided to do my duty and tell you everything."

Margaret Williston's decision was aided by a liberal dose of medicinal lemon gin. I could smell it on her breath.

"Yes, Ma'am. Did they take something else?"

"Well, no. Not really."

"Ma'am?" I asked. I was confused.

"It's my camera."

"They took your camera?"

"No. They used my camera while they were in the house. I had a roll of film in it ... my holiday trip to Mount Pleasant."

Mount Pleasant was a resort about 50 miles east of town where old stiff joints bathed in Mother Nature's warm hotsprings. It was a favored vacation spot for the newly-wed and not-quite-dead. There was nothing to do at Mount Pleasant Resort except bathe in the hotsprings, drink lemon gin and go to bed.

"Okay. They used your camera. Take any good shots?"

"DIRTY FILTHY SCUM-DOGS!" She was not impressed with

my humor. "DIRTY FILTHY SCUM-DOGS!"

The words exploded from her. For Mrs. Williston to refer to people as "dirty, filthy scum-dogs" they must have committed an atrocious crime, although I could see no evidence of the deed.

"Well, Mrs. Williston, if I could see the photographs, it might help me to solve your case."

"If you insist." Margaret left the room and walked into the kitchen. I could hear ice cubes tumbling into a glass. A moment later she emerged carrying an envelope and a renewed smell of lemon.

She handed me the envelope marked White's Photo-finishing. It had a cute picture of a child and a puppy on the front.

I fanned through the photographs. Mount Pleasant Resort. Raccoons eating an apple, three old folks sharing a hot-tub and a young couple kissing. Margaret was a good photographer. I could count the wrinkles.

"Pretty nice shots. My compliments."

"Keep going!" Margaret acknowledged the photographs, especially the one of the young couple kissing. Casually she strolled over to her television and closed her pay-guide.

A couple more raccoons, another hot-tub trio — and there they were! Four pictures. A study in living color of the nude male anatomy.

"I see what you mean. Horrible shots, Mrs. Williston. Just horrible." Inside me the child secretly howled with laughter — and chewed gum.

"The focus is out of wack." The school teacher had obviously scrutinized the photographs carefully before my arrival.

"I hadn't noticed," I apologized. "I can see why you're so upset, Mrs. Williston. But it's only four photographs taken by a couple of hoodlums, three weeks ago."

"Three weeks ago — Yes! That's why I'm so upset!"

"Sorry?"

"See that picture?" The teacher's finger tapped the least offensive photograph. It was a picture of an obese young man. Rear view. His pants were drooped loosely over his ankles and he wore no underwear.

"See that picture?" Margaret repeated.

"Yes." I acknowledged, looking closer.

"It was taken three weeks ago!" She emphasized the time period. "Three weeks ago!"

"Okay."

"And that...." She shook as she pointed to a small pink object, protruding from a large set of pimpled, hairy cheeks.

I acknowledged the rear-view photo and the pink protrusion from the man's rear end.

"Yes." I looked her in the eye. "Can you identify it?"

Margaret Williston began to cry. "It's my toothbrush!"

For the first time in my career I had no comment. As I studied the photograph of her pink toothbrush poking its bristly face from the fat cheeks of an unknown criminal I was shocked. Dear old Margaret Williston had been brushing her teeth for three weeks with a toothbrush which had been secretly held "where no toothbrush had gone before."

What she didn't know was that she was the victim of a perversion practised by young hoods all over North America, but one not generally known. No one with a toothbrush and camera is safe.

Once inside a house, young career criminals search for, among other things, the occupant's camera and toothbrush — or brushes. They then insert the brush — or brushes — into their rectum, photograph the sadistic act and return camera and brush — or brushes — to their original location.

Usually it will be days or even weeks before the poor victim develops the film with its ghastly evidence of warped minds. I sympathized with the weeping Mrs. Williston.

During my career I had learned that this perverted, criminal act was widespread from California to the Arctic — but this was my first encounter. I felt sick.

Cross revolvers awarded for profiency with a hand gun.

CHAPTER SIX

MIDGET TOSSING

Teach a child not to
step on a frog.
It's good for the child —
and better for the frog.

As I climbed back into my police car, I found myself still upset at Margaret Williston's misfortune. I keyed the mike. "Bravo Twenty-Three's 10-8."

"Received Two Three." Sharon's voice again.

"Two Three." I responded.

"Just a reminder ... it's Looney Tunes time at the Last Call."

"10-4. Heading there now."

The Last Call was a beer parlor located in the northern sector of the city. It catered to bikers, perverts and anyone who liked alcohol and hated cops. Every Friday and Saturday night we would circle the pub like Indians circling the wagons. It was another ritual that always gave us some excitement and, once in a while, injuries.

The Last Call was a violent hell-hole. We were under orders never to attend alone and given almost free reign to carry and use our batons. Tonight was special. A midget tossing contest had been advertised in the local newspapers and we all knew there would be standing room only for these Sadistic Olympics. The only winners were the midgets who were paid $5 for each toss they could endure.

As I pulled into the parking lot, a preview of the night's activities was being rehearsed. Two fights were already in progress and one of God's crippled little creatures was limping in my direction. Bow-legged and small, he cradled his left arm and walked like a soldier, dog-tired and battle-weary.

"How's it going, Billy?" I shouted.

Billy Leggens looked up as he walked by my open window. I had first met him when he was arrested at the now-legendary Ewok party.

"Not bad." He walked over to the car. Wincing with pain, he added: "Got me over $300, but I think I busted my arm."

"How so?"

"Big fella tossed me out of the circle and I hit the wall." The crack in the red helmet that hung from his shrunken arm attested to the force of the brutality he had experienced. A broken helmet and two or three X-rays would be his only award for a hard night's work. Billy would quickly spend the money on a woman he was courting ... but he'd always be lonely. He would be broke for a while, too. A broken arm would force him out of the Tossing Circle for at least a month.

"Wonder if they'll toss a cripple?" he asked.

"I doubt it Billy — go get yourself looked after."

"Okay." He turned away.

"Good night, Billy." I watched his small shape shrink into the darkness. It was sad to see a man twice struck down. Once by God, who in his infinite wisdom gave poor Billy a stunted, misshapen body and, secondly, by the disgraceful humiliation of man's violence against his brother.

MIDGET TOSSING CONTEST

The sign over the entrance to Hell was brightly lit. Sick.

Relief was only a briefcase away and my hand blindly felt the familiar cloth wrapping of the Deck. Remove. Unwrap. Shuffle, cut, turn over top card:

> *The boy pokes his stick*
> *at the frog in fun;*
> *But the frog does not take*
> *it in fun —*
> *He takes it in earnest.*

From that night on, Billy would never understand why I called him Froggy — but we were friends and he wouldn't mind. Several years later we would sit together while he explained that his small size landed him many tiny roles in television and the movies. Hollywood North, he called Vancouver, but even at the height of his small-time acting career he would continue to earn a few dollars sacrificing his tiny airborne body to the perverted ecstasy of Midget Tossing.

"It fills a need," was the only explanation my small friend would ever give. I often wondered whose need? It did not seem to matter much to Billy, though. He would soon settle down with a lady and spend the rest of his short life trying to father a child.

FIGHT! FIGHT!

Someone had announced the official closing of the Last Call. Drunks were pushed out the door to settle their grudges in the parking lot. When they ran out of midgets, they turned on each other.

Almost casually, I uncradled my microphone and announced: "Five Bravo Two Three requesting backup at the Last Call. Got some slap-dancing in the parking lot."

"Bravo Seventeen enroute. Be there in three."

The prisoner van was on its way.

"Bravo Six copy. On the way." Stewart Dudzinski was leaving his zone to join in the frolics.

"Bravo Eleven ditto." Bev also invited herself.

What a crew. The Last Call was in for a treat tonight. Rod was driving the van. He liked action and he was still pretty quick for an old cop. Rod was 44 years old. Too old for most cops to still be on the street.

Bravo Eleven — Bev who had parted Wiener from his ear. I wondered out loud if Bev had eaten tonight. To complete the team, Stewart Dudzinski would be pulling up in Bravo Six. Stu was always a treat to watch. Above all, when Dudzinski pulled up, all the police felt just a little bit more secure. Stu had never lost a fight — yet. I waited and watched the fights.

Most people think that Police Officers are trained to wade into the center of a fight and break it up "neat and clean, just like in the movies." Real-life cops are much smarter. They never interfere until the fight is over. After the fight, both warriors are drained of adrenalin and strength. Cleanup is always easier when the competition is tired.

I slid the Deck back into my briefcase. On its return trip, my right hand unzipped the Velcro closure holding the baton in place. I stroked the 16 inches of hard ebony while I waited — and watched!

No one would be hurt too bad. There would be a few teeth left behind, maybe a broken jaw or fist, but the army of fools I was watching were all volunteers. Each one of them had volunteered to numb their brains and abuse their bodies. It was not my job to intervene — too soon. When they were through, we would remove the losers to the comfort of a cement floor and a wise guard. Walter would understand, even if we did not. In the morning they would all be released and Walt would hose down the drunk tank for the millionth time. The large steel drain in the center would carry away the water, the blood and the memories.

Usually only the losers who were left on the asphalt would be arrested. The others would scurry quickly into the darkness like rats. We never chase rats. Fighting with a rat was not on the agenda ... until tonight.

HEADLIGHTS! Bravo Seventeen rolled into the parking lot, followed by two other marked cruisers. Over the loudspeaker mounted on the top of the "taxi of terror," Rod sang two bars from "I Love A Parade," a song he composed just for times like this.

The scene that was about to unfold would be no act of fate, no random occurrence, no unrehearsed play. As a team we would move in tight, locate the hardest, drunkest and toughest trouble-maker we could find and surgically remove him from the crowd. Having done that, awe and respect would still the mob and we would depart unscathed. That was the plan.

But a Police Officer learns early that plans fall apart quickly and adherence to one only limits future options. Often survival meant a savage fight. No rules. Just survival of the fittest.

We were all out of our cars now. Rod tapped his baton nervously in the palm of his hand while Bev fondly stroked Leroy. Stu opened and closed his hands slowly and I just stood there thanking God for the friends He had sent. We were close ... brothers ... even Bev. Few people ever experience the friendship that police officers share moments before a fight. If we were to lose tonight's battle, we would all lose and none of us would walk away. Cowardly cops did not exist on the streets. Not for long. They usually quit or sucked their way into an office job where paper cuts would be their only nemesis. Tonight we shared the fact that anything could happen. Anything but a cowardly act.

Bev flanked on my left, Rod on the right and Stu quietly walked the point. Together we were invulnerable. With Dudzinski's ability to kick, strike or break anything into submission and Bev's ability to cannibalize her opponent, Rod and I had little to fear.

Dudzinski surveyed the crowd for a brief five seconds and recited a poem he rewrote from his childhood. "I spy with my little eye, someone who is...."

"DUSTED! He's Dusted! He's gonna kill someone!" A voice screamed above the others and drew our attention.

William Curtis, all 6'3", 240 pounds, was brutally sinking his boots into an unconscious shape stretched on the macadam. Each kick moved the body a few inches but it barely quivered. Except for the blood which ran freely from a tomato-paste face, there was no signs of life.

Stu made the 50-foot distance in record time, slowing the last second to spin 360 degrees to strike the side of William "Wiener" Curtis' face with the heel of his right foot.

"KEEYAIII!" Karate dictated the use of a blood-curdling call that was meant to strike fear into the enemy's heart, but one-eared Wiener had no heart.

Wiener's head snapped back and blood spurted from the half-ear he had worn ever since the night he had met Bev. Wiener's eyes focused on Stu's still-moving form. Stewart's famous brain-tearing death kick had merely caught Wiener's attention.

"He's dusted!" A voice came from the crowd.

"Shit!" Rod looked worried. Dusted meant that Curtis had snorted, smoked or injected Angel Dust. Phencyclidine. Chemists believed this chemical to be a derivative of piperidine and was commonly used to tranquilize horses, bulls and a few other rowdy animals. On humans it had the opposite affect. Angel Dust had many gifts to offer the human psyche. Wild hallucinations, complete indifference to pain and superhuman strength were the most notable. Wiener was well dusted. Dudzinski's spinning back-kick-to-the-head was only an attention getting tap. It barely registered.

"NEEYAA — KEEEYIII!" This time Stewart's left leg snapped out horizontally, catching the biker's right knee, bending it sideways. Wiener fell hard — then amazingly stood back up.

"We're on fire! We're all on fire!" Curtis launched himself directly at the three of us. In his drug-enriched mind he could see a Hell that we could only imagine. Screaming, he ran to us for escape or vengeance — we weren't sure.

Wiener's hulk travelled faster, gaining speed and momentum. We knew it could not be stopped, even by Stewart the Invincible.

"The things you see when you don't have a shotgun." Rod mouthed the words, stepped forward and volunteered to be the first flea to stop the elephant.

In a move that could never be understood, Curtis stopped short, three feet in front of Rod.

"You're the one! You did this! Now I'll take your bleem!" Whatever a bleem is, it is most assuredly found in a person's throat. In a move like a housewife picking up a tomato at a grocery market, Wiener reached out, took the old veteran by the throat and lifted. As though we had rehearsed the move many times, Bev and I simultaneously moved to the side and stepped forward. Thrusting deeply into Wiener's sides, my baton met Leroy just below Curtis' stomach and just above the small intestine.

"Pop goes the Wiener." Bev loved every minute of this. We released the pressure and waited for Curtis to drop to the ground.

Nothing.

Rod hung onto the madman's wrists and danced the hanged man's waltz.

"C'mon guys. I'm losing it." The words rattled out of Rod's mouth. In the light of the mercury-vapor lamps, the veins on Rod's forehead stood out like small worms.

From behind, Stewart's left arm snapped around Wiener's neck like a whip. Almost as quickly, his right hand snaked around the biker's head and slapped down hard on both his eyes before retracting to complete the noose. Curtis was now blind and unable to breathe.

Rod fell to the ground.

"Dust or no dust — you can't fight without air, asshole!" Dudzinski pulled the noose tight as Wiener's trachea buckled, then closed. The "Japanese Strangle" was brutal but effective. Not as humane as Carotid Control but the Japanese Strangle added one dimension to its effectiveness. Pain.

For the next 30 seconds, Stu rode the back of a drug-crazed bull until Wiener's brain finally went hypoxic and allowed his body to collapse in a twitching, writhing heap. Stu fell with his victim and maintained his grip for another 30 seconds. Later, Stu explained that the extended time spent with his victim was called the "Pit Bull technique." No one argued.

Finally, rising to his feet, Stewart regained his composure.

"The patient's asleep, Doctor. You may proceed." Turning toward Bev, he presented Wiener's motionless body to Bev. She smiled her thanks and stepped forward.

Still smiling, Bev surveyed her prize. Bending forward she pulled her handcuffs from her gun belt and stretched Wiener's right arm into place behind his back. Stu reached down and took the left arm. Half-pulling, half-twisting he rotated the arm until it met its mate. Both wrists were now wearing Bev's bracelets.

It's eerie, the noise a shoulder makes as it dislocates. A muffled POP, followed by a short sucking sound.

Wiener did not even flinch. He was still on fire. Unconscious, but still on fire.

"This is new!" Bev reached down and pulled on her prisoner's pony tail.

"Hey, Cannibal." Rod was still holding his throat. His voice rattled. "Ears are for beginners, think you could swallow a three-foot hair piece?"

Bev looked sideways at Rod. "No, but I can yank it off!" Wiener's body was regaining its awareness as it jerked upwards. Bev tried to make good her boast. She wanted a second trophy to match her ear-jar.

"Whatsa matter sweety? Outa practice?" Stu laughed hard then stepped back and stroked both his ears. Bev made a guttural sound and walked toward the prisoner van, her cargo in tow.

"Oh, no!" Rod ran after her. "Ya can't mix animals and humans. He's going in your car, not the van!"

"Why?" Bev objected.

"He's dusted! Even with the cuffs on, he'll waste the bozos I'm carrying. The man's crazy, got the strength of five men and he's on fire. No way he's coming back to the Crowbar Hotel with me and my guests! It may not be much, but I got a reputation ..." Rod straightened his tie and folded his arms across his chest.

Stu and I had a plan. We raced ahead and threw open the rear driver's side-door of Bev's marked blue and white.

"Drag him over here, cannibal lady. We got a plan!" We rubbed our hands together and winked at Rod.

Bev pulled her catch another 20 feet and released his handle when he was 10 feet from her car. A thud announced the arrival of Wiener's head to the blacktop.

Confirming Stewart's diagnosis, Bev stepped back and announced, "Anaesthesia's in. Shall we begin to operate, Doctor?"

"Air-launch?" Stu asked.

"Air-launch." I confirmed our loading plan.

Rod knew the drill. He'd invented it. Wiener was lying face-down chewing quietly on the parking lot. After Bev had released his head to the pavement he twitched once and rolled over.

"He's in position." Rod stepped up to Wiener's feet and took both pant cuffs in one grasp.

Reaching down, I grabbed William Curtis' right arm and Stu took hold of his left.

"I think we should put this thing back into its socket before launch, feels kinda squishy." Stu reached down and rotated Wiener's arm carefully. "There ya' go partner, good as new." He spoke to the unconscious heap of flesh. "Just 'cause you're some gutter-slime-sleazoid," he looked up sadly, "doesn't mean you ain't human".

"I don't believe this is happening." Bev remarked, almost too embarrassed to acknowledge our plan.

"Body up!" We raised the flesh-rocket three feet and lined it up perpendicular to Bev's awaiting patrol car.

"One ... two ... three!" We called together and, in one move, Wiener's limp body crumpled into the rear compartment of Bravo Eleven.

Unlike Midget Tossing, our launch was out of necessity, not amusement. It was the most effective way of getting a limp body into the soft back seat. Shame entered my mind, though, as I thought of the similarity between us and the midget-tossers I had learned to hate. I could not remove myself from my hatred for the indignity that Froggy and his friends had suffered.

"So what if he wakes up on the way back to the tank? Ever think of that, smart guys?" Bev did not want a madman for company. Curtis was one of the meanest, toughest boneheads we had ever known. Straight and sober he could beat his way out of any police car. If Angel Dust ever gave him the strength to break free of the handcuffs, we would be carrying Bev home in a box. She knew that and so did we.

"No problem." Stu walked to the far side of the car and opened the rear door. Reaching inside, he pulled Wiener's pony tail a full three feet. The body rolled forward and fell to the rear floor of the police car, crammed in tight between the back seat and the aluminum prisoner shield.

"There! He's wedged in tighter than a bull's arse at fly-time!" Stu added. "But just to be sure he doesn't get up...." Dudzinski pulled hard at the braided hair piece, drawing it down and out of the car, over the door sill and under the lower edge of the still-open car door.

"There, that'll hold him real tight 'till you get hungry." He slammed the door hard and almost three feet of hair grew out from the bottom of the crease. "Almost lost you once, Bev."

Stu walked over and placed his arm around her. "Wiener might not like what we've done — I can live with that — but we ain't gonna let him have another go at you. When you get back to the Crowbar Hotel, get some help booking him in, please?"

"Okay," she promised.

Dudzinski released his brotherly grip on Bev and she walked over to the car and opened the door. Looking back she winked, smiled and said, "Thanks guys. Beaucoup thanks!"

Bev slid back into her car and turned the ignition. Looking over her shoulder onto the floor where her prisoner lay twitching, she shoved her head out of the window. "Well, at least you gentleman did something right tonight."

"Hey?" Stu asked.

"You left Wiener's good ear up. Am I hungry!"

Bev pulled her car into gear and drove off into the darkness. Her rear tires chirped on the blacktop as she accelerated out of the parking lot and down the road that only legends travelled.

Rod surveyed the parking lot. It was quiet now. Most of the crowd had cleared out, taking with them Wiener's voluntary victim and any further fun we might have had.

"Good ... no paper work." Stu slapped his hands together. The victim of Wiener's brutal attack had been carried away by his buddies. Since there was no victim or complainant, no charges would be laid and Wiener would be free to walk. The fact that Rod would receive eight stitches for a brutally torn piece of flesh on his throat did not count.

I could still recall the decision handed down by a local judge. It was a decision that empowered drug abusers and reduced the value of a Police Officer's life and well-being.

"A Police Officer elects to pursue a hazardous career. Minor injuries to a policeman are to be expected from citizens rendered insensible by drugs. A police officer should be busy arresting the narcotic sellers, not fighting with the victims of this crime!"

Those simple words rendered the laying of a charge of "Assaulting a Police Officer" near-impossible if the assailant was a drug addict. A judge's words are like a nuclear missile — once launched they become impossible to recall. Within the space of two carelessly worded sentences, Case Law was set and immunity was granted to all the Wieners of the world.

"Minor injuries of a Police Officer are to be expected!" The words still made me feel sick. Stu and I walked over to our cars as Rod drove off slowly. One hand on the wheel, the other holding a flap of skin in place.

Back in my car I heard Rod's voice on the radio.

"Five Bravo Seventeen is R.T.O." — returning to the Office.

"You okay, Rod?" Stewart cared enough to ask.

"Give your head a shake man," was the reply. "It's only a scratch."

"Sorry. Just asking." Stu apologized.

"Bravo Six from Bravo Seventeen." Rod called Stewart's car.

"Six."

"Thanks."

"10-4 buddy. See you at emerg. I'll carp some candies for ya."

"10-4."

The conversation was more like code than slang. Emerg. was the emergency ward of Surrey Memorial Hospital where Rod would go to get his neck stitched. Carp was a nice word for steal. C.A.R.P. meant Creative Acquisition and Redistribution Program. Candies were codeine, a prescription pain-killer that would help Rod sleep tonight. We all knew that Doctor Holler was on duty tonight. Ever since his second conviction for impaired driving, he refused to prescribe pain-killers to police. The nurses were more compassionate, though. They would secretly leave a dozen or so pink tablets out in a prearranged location for us to "steal."

I waved goodbye to Dudzinski as he left the parking lot to carp candies at emerg. Like Alice In Wonderland, life was becoming curiouser and curiouser. Life had become a strange dream. Nothing made sense. Nothing except the trust and friendship shared by four cops in a dimly lit parking lot.

Finally, the neon sign blinked out. Midget tossing over. Sucking in the fresh night air, I reached into my shirt and removed a sweat-softened paper bag.

It was a reminder I didn't need. It was a reminder that somewhere in the Fraser River a lifeless body of an innocent young frog catcher was probably being rolled along the bottom by the current, or snagged in debris along the shore. Meanwhile, his dog waited, hopefully scanning the brown water for her missing companion. Waiting, also, were a mother and a father. They weren't staring at the river, but they were becoming increasingly anxious, hovering between hope and unspoken reality.

Memories of hundreds of faces forced their way into my mind. Fathers, mothers, sisters and brothers — all the families I had ever delivered sad news to visited me in the loneliness of my police car.

There was still work to do.

Sergeant's cloth shoulder patch.

CHAPTER SEVEN

CRIB DEATH

Tell me ... I forget.
Show me ... I remember
Involve me ... I understand.

It was quiet now. Everyone had gone home ... or to jail. Reaching into my tattered leather briefcase, I allowed myself one pleasure. Shuffle. Cut. Turn over top card:

It's easier to fight
for Your principles,
than to live up to them.
Adlai Stevenson

"You're right there, Don." I spoke the words slowly. "You're right." Recalling my disgust at the Midget-Tossing competition, I drew a dark veil across the memory of air-launching Wiener's unconscious body into Bev's car.

I reached for the microphone. "Five Bravo Two Three's 10-8. Anything for me?"

It was nearly 2:00 a.m. No time yet for coffee, and a meal was definitely out of the question. I knew Sharon's computer screen would be lit up with calls so I volunteered.

"Stand-by, Bob. I've got one coming in. Sarge says he wants you to take...."

I did not like the sound of her voice. Sergeant Schlitz rarely interfered with the dispatcher's duties. I feared he was about to send me back to Clarence's home. I wasn't ready for that yet.

"Bravo Twenty-three, ready to copy?"

"Go!" I had already pulled out my pen and notebook.

"Address is seven eight four zero Sechelt Drive. Time in, is one fifty eight. Name is...." Sharon's voice faltered and the air went dead.

"10-9 Sharon?" I asked her to repeat.

"Name's Guilianno, I spell G.U.I.L.I.A.N.N.O. Given one, Mario."

"Received. What ya got, theft of Pizza?" I smiled as I watched the last of the drunks parade from the parking lot.

"It's a crib death, Bob."

The air went dead. For the next few minutes, calls backed up on computer screens, Police Officers checked vehicles and the lucky ones managed to pull into an all-night service station to use the bathroom.

But no one spoke.

"Bravo Two Three copy. Enroute. Ambulance there yet?"

"Just calling them now," Sharon replied.

"10-4. Put me out there in four minutes, Sharon."

"10-4."

Crib Death. Police Officers are trained to face guns, physical attackers and uncaring judges. But nowhere in the R.C.M.P. training does it tell a Mountie how to face a Crib Death.

"Crib Death." The words stuck to my tongue like cold oatmeal.

Police Officers sell their souls. Using their motto: "To Protect and Serve" they volunteer to subject themselves to any human indignity for a paycheck. They rarely complain about anything but

Crib Death.

"10-4, Sharon. Thanks." I held the mike in my hand, wishing I could throw it out the window.

"Sorry, Bob ... Sarge wants you to take this one."

"Tell the Bastard to suck rocks."

"Click ... Click." Sharon keyed her mike twice. The wordless acknowledgment meant only one thing. Sergeant Schlitz heard my last transmission. Hell, I didn't care.

Crib Death.

God in his omnipotence had given mankind many wonderfully hateful things to ponder. On the top of His madness was

Crib Death.

For a reason as yet untold to parent-kind, babies under the age of one year sometimes stop breathing. Permanently. Over the years Crib Death had acquired the rather tacky name of Sudden Infant Death Syndrome. S.I.D.S. for short. But a rose by any other name was still

Crib Death!

I hated this call. I knew what I would be looking at in five minutes. The front door would open quickly after I knocked. Dad would be too grief stricken to talk and Mom would be sitting at the kitchen table, her head held deep in her hands, sobbing ... a box of Kleenex on the table ... five or six wet ones clumped together in front of her. Dad would take me to the room. At the door I would say "Go be with your wife ... I'll see what I can do." Both of us knew I could do nothing.

Five minutes from leaving this parking lot I would walk in the baby's room. Raggedy Ann and Andy would look down from the wallpaper, a Mickey Mouse nightlight would smile up from a floor-level plug socket, and dangling over the crib would be a mobile — stiff pieces of wire all tied together by a thin string, dangling an assortment of shiny butterflies, fairies and birds. Hanging from the center of the mobile would be a small shiny pendant. The pendant would grace the crib and the new life with a nursery rhyme or prayer. This was an Italian family. It would be a prayer.

The child's room would be a collection of smells. Baby powder and Death.

If I was lucky, I would escape this call no wiser for the experience. Older perhaps, calloused most certainly, but no wiser.

I previewed the scene in my mind two more times before I pulled into the Guilianno's driveway. The front porch light cast its dirty yellow glow on the numbers 7840.

The keys slid out of the ignition and clipped themselves to my gun belt. Briefly, I thought of the Deck, of the strength it had given me over the years, then denied its existence. I denied its existence like I denied the reality of the scene I was about to step into.

Thirteen paces to the door. "Knock, knock, knock..." The door opened.

"Hello, Mr. Guilianno, I'm...." Quietly I tried to say my name but it didn't matter. Mario Guilianno stepped aside and held the door open. I walked straight into Hell.

A tired 32-year-old father quietly led the way into the house, through the living room and past the kitchen. Mom was sitting at the table, her head held heavy with grief. The box of Kleenex was where it should be and she had already pushed five or six aside in a wet clump.

I acknowledged her presence, but neither of us could muster the courage to make eye contact.

Mario Guilianno led the tired procession of one down the hallway, past the washroom to a closed door at the end of the world.

At the end of the hall, Mario stopped. He reached out to the doorknob but his hand fell short. Looking down, he quietly spoke. "Angelina's in...." he began sobbing over a sentence he would never complete.

"You go be with your wife ... I'll see what I can do." He turned and walked toward the light in the kitchen.

Scared, sad and angry I turned the knob and walked through the doorway to the saddest place on earth.

The room was dimly lit with a pink elephant lamp on a corner stand. Mickey Mouse smiled on my boots from the plug socket nearest the floor. I hated that smile.

Looking up, I thought the scenery would change. It didn't.

On the wall, over the head of the bed, hung a crucifix. It was placed there to protect Angelina and to remind Mom and Dad that God was looking over their child. Tonight, however, He was busy ... elsewhere.

I looked over the center of the crib. A mobile. Butterflies, fairies and bluebirds.

Dangling from the center of the mobile was a small silver pendant. I walked over to the crib, reached up and turned it to catch the faint glow from the elephant. On one side was an angel — a tiny little creature with wings and a halo. On the other side, I read:

**"The angels gathered o'er your birth
and sang 'go forth, young child of mirth
to live and love - This planet earth.'"**

The floor rose to meet my knees and I found myself beside the crib ... crying.

"COPS DON'T CRY! THEY SHOULD NEVER SHOW EMOTION!" The lesson from the Academy rang around inside my head and I felt sick.

"Cops don't cry!"

I didn't care anymore. I didn't care if I was a cop. I didn't care if I cried and I didn't care about any of the crap that the Academy had beaten into my young eager mind.

It was nearly 3:00 o'clock in the morning. The night had lasted nearly 16 years and if I had earned nothing else in this damned life ... I had earned the right to cry.

I cried.

I cried for all the E.T.'s and Jakes I had ever known, but most of all I cried for little Angelina. Little Angelina would no longer need her diaper changed, she would never fall down and skin her knees and, most certainly, she would never be able to "Live and love this planet earth."

Perhaps neither would I.

Sirens off in the distance. I dried my eyes as they grew louder. I knew help was on its way and, with the added strength that this knowledge brought, I stood up. In a few moments an ambulance with its flashing red and white lights would pull into the Guilianno's driveway. To the entire neighborhood it would announce the departure of an innocent Soul.

I breathed in deep. The smell of baby powder did little to clear my mind. But as I heard the ambulance pull into the driveway I realized I still had a job to do.

Down the hallway I could hear two Emergency Medical Technicians enter the house. They never knocked. Briefly, I wondered what two E.M.T.'s could do to restore life to such a still child. There was no healing to be accomplished here.

"Hello, Bob." Tim and his new apprentice walked into the bedroom quietly. "Anything we can do?"

My head moved slowly, side to side.

"Foul play?" he asked.

"Neg." I reached down and gently rolled Angelina over on her side. "Child appears to be two, maybe three months old, well nourished. Lividity is in place ... I'd say two hours since death. No marks, bruises or signs of mistreatment." I scanned the tiny body from forehead to toes. "Rigor Mortis seems to have commenced in the lower quadrant ... no incongruities. She's...." My throat tightened. "... she's cool, cyanotic...."

"Okay. I'll call the Coroner, get permission to move the ... take her to the hospital."

Tim left the room. His rookie looked at his stethoscope and put it back around his neck. In the next room I could hear Tim dialing the telephone.

Reaching into the crib, I rolled little Angelina's body back to her original sleeping position and carefully tucked in the covers. It seemed like a crime against God to disturb her sleep, looking for bruises or evidence of abuse — but it had to be done. The parents would never know.

The door opened again and Tim walked in. Somehow he possessed a blend of confidence and compassion. "Bob," his voice spoke ever-so-softly. I tried to look in his direction. "I'd like to do something ... with your permission?"

"Oh?"

"Angelina's gone. There's nothing I can do to bring her back, but I'd like to try something."

Hoping against all hope I prayed that Tim could somehow bring life back into a room filled with death.

"Sure." I did not ask what he had in mind. After six years of watching his work, I trusted him.

"The Coroner has given us permission to remove the body." He spoke in whispers. "But there is something I'd like to do first. Follow me."

The three of us walked out of the baby's room, down the hallway and into the kitchen.

Mario and his wife were sitting together at the kitchen table, sharing grief over a pile of wet tissues. In the corner, a kettle was boiling noisily. I left the group and quietly walked over to unplug the kettle. No one would want coffee for a while.

"Mr. Guilianno," Tim's voice blended all the qualities that one normally attributes to a preacher, a family doctor and a friend. "Mrs. Guilianno, I am so sorry ... but there is not very much we can do."

The tears flowed freely from Mom and Dad's eyes as they looked up.

"With your permission we would like to take Angelina to the hospital now."

It was no mistake that Tim refused to mention the words "body" or "morgue." He was trying to give some life back to the house and he chose his words carefully.

"Before we go, would you like a few minutes together with Angelina? I think she would like that."

What was he saying? Angelina wasn't their child anymore. She was a corpse and her corpse belonged to the Coroner. Blue, stiff and dead. A corpse. They didn't want to see their pink sweet-smelling baby all blue and stiff. Was he mad?

"Could we?" Mario dried his eyes and looked at me. I nodded in approval.

"C'mon, Mamma." Slowly they pushed back their chrome kitchen chairs. Mario circled his arm around a crying mother and they quietly disappeared into the darkness of the hallway.

Together.

I watched as the bedroom door closed behind them.

"Sit." Tim pointed to the chairs as he pulled one out for himself.

"Tim," I whispered, "what are you doing? They can't take that! Didn't you see how torn up they were?"

"Truth is, Bob ... you're right. Matter of fact a Crib Death spells the end to most marriages within a year or so. It seems that Mom and Dad usually go through their grief alone. Soon, grief wedges an invisible wall between them and they forget about the love and sharing that brought them together when they first met. I'm just giving them time to share their goodbyes ... and ... maybe something else. Listen." He pointed in the direction of the bedroom.

Through the silence I could hear two voices in Angelina's room. Words forming sentences too sacred to repeat. Tears, sobs and prayers.

Together Mom and Dad prayed for the safe journey of an innocent Soul. They asked God to care for their little Angelina until they could again be together. As we listened, together, I saw Tim's eyes fill with tears. The prayers continued and we listened.

"We forgive you, God, for we do not understand your ways. We will not ask the impossible, Angelina is with you now and she will not come back to us in this house, but we ask you for the strength of her love to remain. Perhaps some day she will have a sister or a brother who will play here ... if you grant it. But we ask that you leave us with the love she gave us. Her visit was too short, Lord, but help us to remember her love. Please?"

They forgave God? I had never thought of that. What if God was not perfect? What if He made mistakes?

What if God cried?

All my life I had been taught that God was All Knowing, All Powerful and Always in Charge. If tragedy struck, it was because He had planned it. When we did not understand tragedy, it was because we were too stupid to understand His Master Plan. I had never thought that God could make a mistake.

What if God cried?

Could we ever learn to forgive Him? Could I?

There in a lonely kitchen that night, in the midst of anger and tears, I had learned everything a cop ever needs to know. I had learned that life was not a matter of alleging blame but a process of forgiveness. Of growth. Of Love.

Why had they never taught this in the Academy? All our lessons had been on the use of force and control! Nothing was ever mentioned on the subjects of love and forgiveness.

Then I remembered the words spoken in a classroom a long time ago — in a land filled with short-haired, stiff-spined recruits. Words spoken by a friend, Corporal Withers:

"Before you leave my class you had better learn one thing! This Police Academy is of little value except to teach you to march, salute and run 'till you drop in your own vomit. If you are to survive, forget about your bullshit Scarlet Tunic, your high-brown boots and Stetson and learn that life as a cop is a series of lessons and you had better be damned good students!"

Corporal Withers had spoken the truth. I was living in a world where we are given all the tests first and the lessons later. I had graduated from the Academy and passed my exams. My lessons were taking place now! I was sitting the final exam that Don Withers had often spoken of. The fact that I was a member of the Royal Canadian Mounted Police no longer mattered to me. The Scarlet Tunic and the high-brown boots were only a costume. They would serve a post card or a statue in a souvenir shop better than they would serve me. I was no longer a cop. Instead, I was in training to be something much more important. A person. With feelings.

Lost in my own personal world, I had not noticed the moment when Angelina's parents had returned. As Mr. Guilianno plugged in the kettle I found myself nodding in acceptance to his offer of a cup of coffee.

Three years later I once again met the Guilianno family in a nearby park. With both arms full of seized beer from a group of rowdy youths I acknowledged a couple passing by — with a stroller. Mrs. Guilianno recognized me and we talked as if friendships had not been interrupted by a three-year gap. I awkwardly held Timmy, their three-month-old baby.

He was named after a compassionate paramedic.

I was out of the house. The red and white ambulance lights grew small in the distance and I pulled out of the Guilianno's driveway slowly. Reaching for the mike I spoke clearly: "Bravo Twenty-three's 10-8."

Loudly and plainly, I announced my willingness to take calls. Partly because I was happy to be away from little Angelina's room and partly because something inside had given me an understanding, a confidence that I had never experienced at any time in my life. I was back in service, perhaps more 10-8 than I had ever been before.

"10-4. Thought we'd lost you for a while." Sharon answered. Somewhere in the confusion of tears and the making of a friendship three hours had slid by.

"Sorry, Sharon. Any calls backed up? My apologies for taking so long. Tell Sarge I'm sorry. Why didn't you telephone the house?" I listed my questions in quick-fire random order.

"My screen's clear. Sarge said to leave you alone." She answered the important questions and ignored the others.

"10-4. Tell him I owe him one."

"I know you do." Schlitz had picked up Sharon's microphone and told the truth.

"Don't forget about our date. Zero-Six-Hundred. My office." Schlitz's voice had softened from what I could remember.

"Zero-Six-Hundred hours. My office." The words still bounced around inside my tired head. I was politely being reminded to attend my own execution.

Quietly, I drove away from the Guilianno's. It was nearly five-thirty and the pre-dawn sun had washed away all the night-time stars. Looking up into the pre-dawn sky, I regretted not having a star to wish upon. In a stranger's house I had just met a friend. In the presence of Death, I had just begun Life. And in the midst of tears, I had just heard two people pray for happiness.

I didn't care about the fishbowl. I cared about Clarence and a sunrise that would only bring his parents and I together.

Numbed with pain, I drove south on Sechelt Drive.

Damn, I hated sunrises.

CHAPTER EIGHT

FROGS, DOGS AND PROMISES

Worry is the darkroom
where negative thoughts
are developed

The sky was becoming brighter. A natural occurrence for this time of day. It had been 11 hours since Schlitz had embarrassed me in front of the entire world. Eleven hours that had flashed by like a succession of scenes from an old "B" movie. No plot. No story. Just scenes.

I was tired. Eleven hours tired. In the time-space of one short shift I had seen a broken arm (I wonder if Batman really signed his cast?), some excellent photography (I wonder what they did with her dental floss?), a Good Year wiener Roast (I wonder if Jake is asleep yet?), a flying drunk (I wonder if Wiener is awake yet?) and....

Five thirty. The sun was punching its way through the horizon to light up another day. I would sleep through most of this one, hopefully.

Five thirty. I smiled a sleepy smile as I squished my eyelids and watched the sun announce its arrival to a fearful world. Inside my head played a movie of a missing boy, a sad dog, worrying parents and a job left undone.

"Bravo Two-Three, you 10-6?" Sharon had obviously overheard my thoughts and interrupted the mental movie with a question.

"Neg. Sharon. Just one call to finish."

"10-4. I was just going to remind you."

"Tom back at the office yet?" I hoped against all hope.

"Negative, he's still coded 'at scene,' been trying to reach him but I guess his portable's dead."

"10-4. Mark me 10-7 in Mayberry in about 10 minutes would you? I'll go back and wait with the parents."

"Received Two-Three." The air went quiet.

"Bob?" Sharon's voice queried.

"Two-Three," I answered.

"Good Luck," she said. Again the air went quiet.

I headed east along a road paved with tears, fears and wishes I'd never been born. At least the road had a destination ... not like the path that Clarence had so recently followed.

The morning sun shone hard into my eyes but the pain was nothing like I knew I would feel when I held Clarence's mother in my arms and told her we were calling out our Dive Team. I needed a friend but my police car was empty. Briefly I thought of calling Sharon on the radio but the lump in my throat would not allow that. I reached out, rested my hand on the mike and clicked the button twice. "KSSHHHT. KSSHHHT."

"KSSHHHT. KSSHHHT." Someone answered. Two mike clicks was an unspoken code. It was used when police cars passed each other on the street or anytime one officer wanted to tell another "you are not alone." It helped a bit.

Dealing with the next of kin was the worst part of being a Police Officer. All the bruises, cuts and stitches I had taken over the years had left insignificant scars compared to those inflicted by the sorrow of telling Mom and Dad "Your son's not coming home today. Or perhaps it was a daughter, or husband or wife or sister or brother...."

On the way back to Mayberry I turned left ... and detoured down Memory Lane. Maybe I would find an answer there.

I was a recruit again. Sitting, eagerly watching an old scratchy 16-millimeter movie. I was fresh and alert. Video had not yet been invented.

"Chance of a Lifetime", the title of the movie read in large, gothic, red-dripping letters. In the next 30 minutes we would witness the birth of a child. In a neatly packed 30-minute parcel of controlled madness, 32 junior police officers would learn how to deliver a baby in the back seat of their police car. The lesson was graphic and simple and came to us in a three-point resume.

Corporal Withers dictated the notes we would need to pass our written exam:

POINT ONE: Childbirth is natural and will occur without your help. Do not interfere! Let the woman do all the work!

POINT TWO: Tie off the umbilical cord and cut it six to twelve inches from the baby!

POINT THREE: Save the afterbirth. Wrap it up separately and give it to the doctor at the hospital!

Corporal Withers emphasized the last point as if it were triple-scored on his lecture notes. We were never told why it was so important to "save the afterbirth!" but it made good sense. Throwing it out the car window was definitely out of the question and taking it home would most certainly shorten an already stressed marriage. Somewhere in the back of my demented mind I pictured a doctor secretly hoarding a lifetime collection of placentas in large canning jars. No reason — just a picture that had appeared — perhaps for the sole purpose of reminding us to "Save the Afterbirth!"

Don Withers concluded the lesson with one sentence:

"It is unlikely that any of you will experience the miracle of birth, but if you do — save the afterbirth and let God do the rest."

Then he added quietly. "Yesterday we took five minutes during our Human Relations class to tell you how to deliver a death notification to a family. If any one is interested, come to my house tonight and I'll tell you the truth." He scrawled his address on the blackboard. We copied this information into our notebooks. Andre Bryant, the gentle giant, nodded in my direction, acknowledging there would be at least two of us who would take Don up on his offer.

Later than night, Andre and I sat, transfixed by stories of grief and sadness. Although he was out of uniform, somehow Don Withers seemed more imposing, more knowledgeable, more human than we had ever perceived him to be.

Over cookies and coffee graciously served up by his beautiful wife, Don told us what our lives would be like when we knocked at a door at four o'clock in the morning to deliver the bad news. Memories of a miracle birth were washed from our minds as we engraved a new set of instructions.

"When you walk through the door and deliver the sad news that a loved one has passed away," Don looked down for a moment, then up towards the stipple ceiling of his living room, "leave your badge and all that Mountie-stuff behind."

He drew a deep breath.

"You have been taught to maintain and control your surroundings at all cost and at all times. Forget that! It's crap! You have also been taught not to get involved in the pain of others. Forget that, too!" He looked into our eyes, like a friend who wishes to share a secret.

"It is through the miracle of birth or the tragedy of death that you will find yourself ... or lose yourself ... forever." Don looked at a small index card he had laid on the table.

In order to be Human,
you must first do —
a Humanitarian Act.
Jose Silva

Andre and I left Don's house that night, embarrassed to have been the only two in our troop to take him up on his offer. Recruits were never allowed to socialize with their instructors, and off-duty meetings was a punishable offense for both the recruit and the instructor. We were the only two who did not care about rules and Don was the only instructor in the Academy who knew better than those who wrote the rule book. We were a small family.

Driving back to the base was a quiet time for both of us. As I parked my 1958 red and white Dodge near the Drill Hall, I could hear Andre repeat the words softly.

"In order to be Human, you must first do a Humanitarian Act."

I wondered which one of us would be first.

I was still wondering when I crested the Wolfe Creek Bridge. Two minutes to Clarence's house. Two minutes to Hell!

In spite of my wishes, time would not stand still. It would not even slow down. Fate steered my patrol car onto a gravel driveway — clear into a morning sun that I would never forget.

"A man has to do what he has to do." An old cliche given to me by my brother rattled around inside my head as I walked reluctantly up to the front door. Gently I reached out and tapped my arrival.

No answer.

The impossible chance of a quick coward's retreat flashed into my mind. I knocked louder.

The door opened.

"Officer? Have you....?" Mr. Henderson hoped against all odds that Clarence would be sleeping in the back of my patrol car. He hoped against all odds that with my arrival, he would take his sleepy dragon-slaying, frog-catching son gently in his arms and tuck him into his bed. And he hoped against all odds that he would have to tell Clarence that "All the dragons in the world aren't worth scaring the britches off your Mother."

Mr. Henderson hoped against all odds.

Sadly, I knew that Clarence was sleeping. I could feel it in my soul. I didn't much believe in that psychic stuff I had been told over one-too-many-beers by a friendly instructor in a land far, far away. But once in a while I discovered that if I could bring a problem clearly to mind, an answer would accompany it.

Clarence was sleeping. I knew that. My throat tightened at the sight of his still-wet body and I rejected the image. Denial was still working bravely inside me, even if understanding had taken a holiday.

"Come in, Officer." I followed Mr. Henderson through the front door, down a hallway and into the kitchen. The floor plan of this house was almost identical to the Guilianno's. From the strained coffee cup and the box of Kleenex on the kitchen table, it became apparent that Mom and Dad had been up all night. Waiting for Clarence.

"Mr. Henderson ...." The words I knew I had to say stuck in my throat.

"Yes?" He answered. Meg poured me a cup of coffee. She held it out and I accepted it with a thankful nod.

Damn. Why can't she see what's happened to her son? Why can't she just give herself the bad news? Why didn't she know that the only part of her son I could ever return to them was a stupid brown paper bag I still carried under my shirt. I unfastened one button, reached in, then changed my mind.

Tillie had crept up to my side. I reached down and petted her soft head. She knew what had happened. Was she the only one?

"Tillie. Go lay down!" Dad spoke the command.

"No, it's okay. I used to have a dog just like her," I lied. "Please let her stay."

"You're gonna get dog hair all over your blue pants," Mrs. Henderson warned.

Kneeling down beside Tillie, I held her close. I didn't care. I would have gladly taken all of her hair and left her bald. If only....

"Mr. and Mrs. Henderson, we have been trying to reach Tom, our Dogmaster, for the past six hours. I guess he's developed some type of problem with his portable radio but...."

They looked on. Innocently, they could not know or understand what package fate was about to deliver to their door in the next few minutes. Neither did I.

"Well," I continued, "usually Tom only tracks for an hour or so but tonight I guess he is just trying a bit harder." I could feel Tillie's warm dog-body push closer. I turned away from the parents and spoke to Tillie.

Quietly, Tillie and I shared a few private thoughts. Her soft eyes looked up and told me everything would be okay but I could not see clearly. Tears began to fill my eyes and I held back a sob.

Tillie understood. She understood everything. In her soft brown eyes I could see the same sadness that I had seen in Angelina's parents. Loneliness. I looked beyond the loneliness and as Tillie's eyes raised to meet mine, I also saw understanding and forgiveness. I knew that after I had left this house, Tillie would remain, standing by the parents. A guardian of love.

Dogs never questioned, never demanded and never held a grudge against life, fate or even God. They asked only to be loved and promised only to be loving. Whatever God Tillie prayed to was certainly wiser and more loving than the one I had been shown as a child.

I had turned my back on Clarence's mother and father to seek the comfort of a dog's soft face and brown eyes. It felt good. The pain that came with the job was slowly subsiding as I scratched Tillie's ear. She pushed hard into my hand, wagged her tail and let out a soft moan.

"She always does that when Clarence scratches her ears," Meg explained. "Just wait 'till he gets home. That dog's going to lick his face-off!"

I stood up. Tillie leaned tight against my leg. It was time to face life — head on.

I drew strength from a card I had crumpled, years ago, in a fit of rage:

Imagine your world —
Perfect in every way.
Then be humbled, for God
has already imagined it
Much better.

As a child I could remember wishing upon a star. The adult I had become briefly wished upon a card. An old crumpled card:

Would the child you were
be proud of the man —
You Have Become?

My world was about to crumble. I needed help. I breathed in deeply and faced Clarence's parents. Tillie watched, hoping I could do this right.

"Mr. and Mrs. Henderson, we haven't heard from Tom for over six hours. He's our best Dogmaster. Usually, if Tom can't pick up a trail in an hour or two, there's no trail to be found."

Mom and Dad did not understand. I tried to ease the pain by explaining Clarence's fate in small stages.

"The river out back. Clarence played there often, didn't he?"

"Sure does," Meg agreed. She did not even realize I had used the past tense.

Tillie whined. Then barked.

"Sshhh — " I tapped her nose. Death notifications should be a quiet time. A time of truth. A time of closeness, honesty. A time of....

BANG!

The front door flew open.

"Hello? Anybody home?" I knew the voice. It was Tom's. Damn, he couldn't have come at a worse time.

"Hello? I'm sort of wet ... don't want to walk on your new carpet. Anyone home?"

"C'mon in. Don't worry 'bout the carpet," Mr. Henderson hollered back.

"Tom?" I called out his name loud enough for him to hear but soft enough to convey a hidden message.

"Tom, I'm...." As I turned toward the hallway I saw the first angel-sent-from-God I had ever seen. Well, it wasn't really an angel! It was a six-year-old, soaking wet dragon-slayer. He was proudly trailing behind him a large orange plastic bag.

"Got us some big ones, Tillie!" Clarence knelt down and hugged his companion. Tillie whined and squirmed in excitement as the bag opened and poured out its contents in all directions.

Frogs!

Large, small, green, brown and spotted.

Frogs!

There in a small country kitchen, time stood still long enough for everyone to experience the magic of tears, miracles and —

Frogs!

Clarence was home. I looked at Tom. He was crying. Clarence's parents were also blinded with their own tears of joy as they held their son in a three-way embrace.

And Tillie? Tillie was busy herding

Frogs!

Two cups of coffee and an eternity later, Tom had told the story of a young boy who had abandoned his paper bag for a large plastic "Tuf-Guy." He had ventured out too far on a forbidden wharf and fallen in. Buoyed up by the air trapped in the large plastic garbage bag, Clarence finally washed ashore a "mile or so" downstream.

Clarence was a brave young lad. He could face up to dragons, demons and even to monsters that lived under his bed. Coming home wet, though, was something to be feared by even the bravest of heroes.

"He was hiding in the Spencer's barn," Tom explained. "I knew Smokey had a track but with all the cows and chickens it was confusing. If I'd listened to him and watched closer, we'd have brought Clarence home sooner." Tom watched Clarence as he told his story.

"Finally, Smokey dragged me over to that old brown barn and I found Clarence, all crumpled up in a corner. He was sleeping."

We all listened to Tom's miracle tale as he continued. "That was about four o'clock." He added.

"Why didn't you call in earlier, Tom?" I asked the question carefully not to destroy the magic we could all feel.

"'Cause I fell in the river half an hour before I found Clarence. Think your Dive Team could find a radio for us? It's about a mile downstream from here."

I knew they could.

"But the Spencer's is only about a mile or so west of here. How'd it come to take you two hours to walk back?" I asked as Clarence's Dad looked up. He was about to ask the same question.

"Frogs!"

"Huh?"

"Frogs!" Tom looked at the floor and laughed.

"Frogs. You see, Clarence was too afraid to come home. He knew you'd be upset with him. It was a chore just to remove him from the barn, then once we got outside the barn I saw what we needed."

"Frogs?" I asked.

"Frogs. Clarence told me that you, Mrs. Henderson, promised him, if he ever caught 12 frogs, he would get to make a wish. You also promised him that his wish would come true. Well, you can count them if you like."

Tom looked down at the floor. "But I see by the way you two are holding him that his wish has just come true." Smiling through a set of brown misty eyes, Tom added: "All is forgiven, is it not?"

Uniform hat badge with cloth backing.

CHAPTER NINE

THE TONTINE

We must give up
What we are,
In order to discover
What we might become!

I drove away from Mayberry that morning feeling fresh, renewed, different.

The world had not changed. The sunrise was the same as all the sunrises I had seen for the past 16 years, yet everything was different. I thought of the card I had crumpled in anger ... the one that told me that God had imagined the world more perfect than I could. My deck had 51 cards. Before I went to bed this morning I would reunite that card and put it back into the deck. It was true. Truth should never be thrown away.

Easing the pressure on the accelerator, I let my police car slow to 20 miles an hour. I wanted this journey to last. Tom and Smokey had brought us together to share a moment, an island in time. I wasn't ready to leave that Loving Place, not yet. Not for the rest of my life.

The sun was warm, the robins and starlings were calling in the day and the farm smell of Mayberry was "fragrant-cow." But it was beautiful.

The mist that had gathered in my eyes softened the shadows and the picture I saw was more beautiful than anything ever painted by a master. It was delicious.

The picture I was driving into was certainly painted by a Master Artist.

I drove my blue and white into that picture. It was a picture of a perfect world. I vowed never to return to the hate-tainted, guilt-ridden reality I had left behind. For once in my life, everything was okay. The past, what I felt inside, even my future. I did not know what it was, but it was okay.

Every day is created perfect.
The imperfection lies only —
In what we do with it.

The card superimposed itself over my new world. Corporal Withers was right! Marvelous! Just bloody Marvelous!

"KSSHHHT." The radio came to life. "Bravo Twenty-three, you 10-8?" Sharon's voice did not pull me out of my daydream. This was my new reality. I invited her in.

"10-4 Sharon. I'm more 10-8 than I have ever been before!"

"Good!" A male voice took over the microphone. "Remember our date. I'll be here when you pull in."

"10-4, Sarge. I'm looking forward to it." I cradled the mike and smiled. No torturous, blister-popping, skin-peeling reaming-out ever planned could spoil my new world. I was invincible. "Let him try. That ol' fart ain't got no power over me. Why, if he tries giving me a rough time I'll...." My brain stopped talking.

What do you do with a Sergeant bent on destruction. In his hands he held a pen. He often used that pen as a threat. "You signed three oaths with a pen," he would remind us all-too-often. "A pen brought you into this outfit and with a pen I can take you out!" His words were powerfully true. My mind raced ahead to the time I would spend in his fishbowl this morning. My heart sank.

"Okay, Bob," I mouthed the words. "It's time to try out your brave new world. Remember your promise! Live every day as if it were created — perfect!" I was rehearsing the next few hours, considering all possibilities and all possible outcomes, good and great. I took a few moments to listen to my new brain talk to me.

"If he tries giving me a rough time, I'll invite him into my new world!"

I knew the envelope that Sergeant Schlitz had given me was a Ten-o-Four. I knew I would be asked to acknowledge the written reprimand for "daydreaming during briefing" and I knew I was in trouble — serious trouble — all over a trivial incident.

I also knew our meeting would be concluded with a simple admonishment: "This will now serve as a permanent part of your career. I'll place it personally on your service file. I expect much more from a young fella like you. Frankly, son, you disappoint me." The last words spoken were planned to make me feel bad, guilty, ashamed.

On the way back to the office I vowed never to return to the old world behind me. It was not a very nice place that I had come from. Ulcers lived there. Ulcers and Sergeant Schlitz. Instead, I would invite Sarge to join me in my new world. Who knows. Maybe?

Preparing myself mentally and physically, I pulled the police car over to the side of the road and reached into my briefcase. Retrieving the envelope I had been handed at the beginning of shift, I tore one end open and slid out the single sheet of paper it held. I was ready to read the insult and sign it prior to our meeting. Hopefully, this simple act would shorten my punishment. With a short blast from a fiery Sergeant I stood a chance of escaping the inevitable "Just-so-it's-clear-in-your-mind, I'll-read-this-to-you" phase of our meeting.

I unsheathed the green-lined page from its envelope.

"BOB. PLEASE SEE ME BEFORE YOU GO OFF-SHIFT. PLEASE."

Schlitz had never said please in his entire life.

Not quite understanding what surprise was waiting for me, I drove off quickly into my new world. I was not frightened or intimidated anymore. I had left those emotions behind.

But I was puzzled.

PLEASE?

It was six-thirty when I unloaded my police car. The office smelled of coffee and fatigue. Nodding at the other officers, we silently said good morning as they left and I stayed late.

My mind had already gone home and I was left alone to slay a dragon more fierce than any monster Clarence had ever encountered. Tom had arrived just ahead of me. We stopped and faced each other 10 feet inside the door.

"Tom," I spoke his name quietly. Tom smiled a wet smile. "Thanks," was all I could push out.

"Ya." He answered. Both our eyes filled as I knelt down to face Smokey.

"And you, you fur-lined miracle. Goooood Boooooy!" I gave Smokey the best present a police service dog could ever receive. Praise. Loud, clear and from the heart.

"Gooooood Boooooy!"

Smokey barked a dog thank you.

After letting Smokey enthusiastically wash my face, I laughed. I looked at Tom. Tom looked at me. Smokey looked at both of us. Two eyes focusing in different directions and we all laughed. Together. The three of us.

Words were not needed. We watched each other's face. Tired friends. Smokey understood.

A minute later six tired, wet legs walked silently away into the morning. "C'mon, Son," Tom said. "Gonna be a special breakfast for you when we get home!"

Alone, I walked a few feet to a small window, passed in my shotgun and portable radio and waited.

"You want something?" The voice on the other side of the counter spoke.

"No signature — no portable or gun." I pointed to the sign reminding us both that everything required a signature. He grumbled and signed the duty log.

"Damned Dogmaster, lost another radio. Son-of-a-bitch couldn't find his arse in a telephone booth with both hands."

I left his words hanging in the air as I turned to walk towards Sergeant Schlitz's office. No longer would I accept anything negative into the new world I had entered. I stopped briefly at the door and leaned forward to look in. Submissively, I tapped at the door frame.

"Huh?" Schlitz looked out over his half-glasses.

"Sarge, I...." He held his hand up to stop me.

"Damned paper work. Five minutes to catch a shit-rat and five hours to write a report." Schlitz closed the bulky file he was brooding over and spun his chair to face me head-on.

BLOOD!

Favoring his left arm, Schlitz threw the paper file into a wire basket and stood up.

"Sarge. Your arm. You okay? What...?"

"Not here!" Leaning down, he reached into his canvas duty bag and retrieved a small package. He winced.

" 'Bout time we talked. Been meaning to do this for a long time. C'mon pard, the fishbowl's no place for us. Grab your briefcase and follow me."

I was shocked. He knew his office was called the fishbowl. How could he? No one could have ever said that to his face. I followed my boss down the corridor, turned right and climbed two sets of stairs. At the top I caught up to him and he nodded in the direction of the Chief's office.

"It's Sunday morning. We'll use the Old Man's office. Rumor has it he was quite a guy in his day. I think old Heck would be happy if we put his office to some good use. Let's break with tradition and use his office — shall we?" I nodded as I followed him towards the Chief's door.

Inside the Chief's office, Schlitz slumped into a chair and held his arm close to his body. Tired, he looked up at me. "Coffee?" He asked.

"You bet! I'm buying."

"I know." He frown-smiled. "Thanks. I'll just rest here a minute."

I turned and walked out the door, across the main administrative office to a hallway. Something was different. Strange. Wonderfully good. I didn't know what it was.

I sacrificed 50 cents to a brightly lit machine which promised "each cup freshly brewed". My hand reached out and pushed three buttons. EXTRA CREAM. EXTRA SUGAR. EXTRA STRONG. Repeating the process a second time, I wondered: "That's it. He's different. In one shift he said 'please' and 'thanks.' What the Hell was happening?"

Deep inside I held tight to a prayer that told me what was about to happen would have nothing to do with Hell. I prayed to a new God. A short prayer. It was my first attempt at living.

"Let this be good, God. Please let this be good." Looking up at the dirty ceiling, I added "...'cause I'm buying the coffee!" I still thought God needed a reason to be good.

Juggling two extra strong coffees, I balanced my way down the hall, across the tile floor and into the Chief's office. Softly kicking the door closed with my right foot, I reached down and sat a coffee next to Schlitz. His eyes were closed.

"Sorry, sort of drifted off. The insides of my eyelids are looking pretty good right about now."

"Ya." I sat down next to him.

"Sarge, you okay?" I had to ask.

"Remember Jim Bretton's store?" He spoke slow.

"Ya — been robbed a zillion times. I was there last night, for a few minutes."

"I know. Just like you to visit the store every night and set up a routine."

I cocked my head, wondering what he was getting to.

"Remember your conversation with Inspector Craig?"

"How could I forget it. Him and his damned overtime budget. If he'd sprung a few bucks for more manpower instead of pleasing the politicians, we...."

"Just hold on there." He interrupted me. "After you left my office, I got to thinking."

"About?"

"About how you young fellas represented everything I was — and can never be again."

"I don't know 'bout that Sarge. At least you have a reputation."

"Ya. That and 50 cents will buy you a cup of this monkey-pee." He raised the cup to his lips and winced with the pain.

"Well, I'll ramble on here, make a long story longer. While you were sitting in front of Jim's store, I got to thinking. Thinking about the way things used to be." He paused and set his cup on the oak table. "And wondering where we went wrong."

"I don't know about that." I tried to console his guilt by lying. He didn't even acknowledge my comment.

"So I changed clothes and climbed into an unmarked." Taking another sip of monkey-pee, the old has-been straightened himself in the chair. "About the time you drove out of the parking lot, I was pulling into the rear alley.

"Ya?"

"Ya. I went into Jim's store and read skin books for two hours.

Man, those pictures sure are getting filthy. Disgusting! I guess I'm just getting too old to understand these things." He shook his head in disbelief.

I looked at Schlitz straight on. It was obvious he did not call me here to talk about his recent sex education.

"So?" I prompted him to continue his story.

"So, I leafed through the porno pictures for over two hours." He dragged out the suspense.

"And?"

"And some greasy-assed shit-head walks in with a sawed off 12-gauge shotgun and asks Jim to empty his register."

"So you...?"

"So I plays by the Marquis of Queensbury rules and shouts 'Police — drop your gun!' and he ain't heard of any rule book governing the etiquette of armed robbery. Son of a bitch shot me!" He sipped his coffee again, more noticeably this time.

"Then I empties my gun on him. Only hit him once but a man sure goes down fast when you splash his kneecap all over the potato chip rack. Squeals kinda loud, too!"

"You son-of-a-bitch!" I complimented him in a way only a cop could understand.

"Thanks!"

"You okay?"

"Ya. Only took two pellets. Aches like Hell. You got any candies in that old leather sack of yours?"

Remembering the three ribs I had cracked when a drunk fell on me a month ago, I reached into my briefcase and offered up my last two painkillers. My ribs still hurt but I always tried to avoid painkillers. My stomach didn't like them either.

"Thanks." He rolled them on his tongue, coated them with spit and pounded them down with a large gulp of hot, brown extra strong, then washed that down with another.

"Sarge. Why didn't you tell us?"

"And wreck your routine. No, sir! I figures this hair-ball is casing the joint. Soon as you leave he'll wait a spell then try a hit. Besides," he added, "I just wanted to prove something to myself."

"You didn't have to." I again tried to console him, but he wasn't hurting, he was proud.

"Yes, I did." A smile over took his face. A serious smile.

"To you!" I raised a white styrofoam cup and toasted a friend.

"To me!" He drank with me.

That was the day I'd made a new friend and found respect for an old adversary. Together, Sergeant Schlitz and I quietly finished our coffee. Few words were spoken as he waited for the codeine to take away the pain.

"Sarge?"

"Ya."

"Why'd you give me that Ten-o-Four? Said on it you wanted to meet me before I went home this morning. Couldn't have been to tell me about your shoot-out. You wrote it before I ... uh ... we left the office."

Schlitz's face grew somber. Serious. Sad.

"I've been hearing 'bout a Deck of cards you carry with you. You don't talk much for a young fella but I heard you got a special attachment to them.

"Ya." I acknowledged the truth and looked down at my battered brown leather briefcase. Home for a deck of cards.

"Earlier this morning ... last night ... when you were in the fishbowl, you spoke of a man named Withers."

"Uh huh."

"Tell me about him."

Drawing on a memory that was both happy and sad, I spoke Don's name. I used words like Master, Hero and Friend. A caring friend. The stories from my Academy days unfolded and, as I spoke, Schlitz smiled.

"And the deck of cards?"

"The Deck has taught me everything I ever wanted to know. It answers my questions, keeps me company and forces me to look at life. Honestly. It keeps me going when I want to quit. Corporal With... Don, gave it to me as a going-away present. Asked me to remember him everytime I read his words. He...."

"His words?"

"Ya, his words. It ... well...." I paused long enough for a memory to come back clearly. The gift was Don's. The inspiration and the memories I had were of Don, but as I brought back the memory of our meeting-under-the-stars one cold winter night, his words came back to me as clear as the Centurion's stars which hung over our heads. I remembered the origin of the cards was not with Don. It was a gift he had exchanged with a friend. A friend he had when he was a recruit. A friend who shared and cared with him.

"No. I guess these weren't his words." I reached into my bag and held the Deck out for Schlitz to see. "I remember Don telling me about the night he and a troop-mate each made a deck of 52 cards. Then they traded decks and promises of eternal friendship."

All these years I had given Don Withers credit for the wisdom contained in the Deck. The gift was his — but the words belonged to someone else. A stranger I had never met.

These weren't his words! "It was his troop-mate!" I whispered the words loudly.

"That handkerchief you got them wrapped in. It's old enough to be an antique." Sarge's eyes grew tired as he gazed at my Deck.

"It is." I unwrapped the cards and, for the first time ever, I inspected the yellow-stained hanky. In the corner was a tattered monogram.

"S.S." I read the initials out loud.

"First name Sterling." Sarge looked at me.

"You know this man?" I asked. The cards felt heavy all of a sudden.

"Sterling Schlitz." He smiled the kind of smile that grows on your face when you meet a friend after a hundred year separation.

I was to be one of the few officers who would ever learn Schlitz's first name.

"You? You and Don?"

"Don was my troop-mate. Together we endured nine months of hardship, loneliness and R.C.M.P. brainwashing. Together we vowed we would always remember the pain and never forget our friendship." Tears rolled freely down Sterling's face. No one had ever seen him cry.

"Here." I held out the old hanky. "I think you dropped this a long time ago."

"Thanks."

Sterling Schlitz cleared his throat and wiped his eyes. I placed the Deck in front of him. He cut the Deck and turned over the top card:

The man who judges,
doesn't matter —
Because the man who
matters ... never judges.

We smiled. Somewhere in the room, an invisible spirit shared our smile. It was Don Withers.

Sterling reached into his shirt pocket and handed me a package. An old handkerchief carefully folded over a deck of cards.

"I think Don would want you to have these."

In the corner of the coffee-stained cloth, a monogram: "D.W."

"This one's 'bout worn out. It's time you started on a new Deck and I thank you for the return of mine." Sterling winked. "Besides, there's something we have to do now."

"Do?" I asked.

"Don and I," he said, as he looked at his own Deck of cards.

I held my new Deck carefully. It felt strange. Wonderfully strange. What new wisdom did it contain? Would it help me through life's bumps and burns as Sterling's Deck had done? I was almost fearful of consulting this Deck. I didn't know it well enough to trust my life with it. Not yet.

For 36 years I had resisted the only thing that life constantly offers. Change.

I feared the fork in the road that this new Deck would offer and I set it down on the table in front of me. I did not realize I had already made a decision and taken a new path at the Hendersons' home. I smiled. Like a delayed entry in a computer, Sterling's last words cleared through my mental clutter and registered on my brain.

"Besides, there's something we have to do now."

I looked at my new friend. He was sorting through his Deck. Searching.

"When Don and I made our Decks, we each double-sealed one card. A tontine was established that night in the barracks."

"Tontine?" The word was new to me.

"Tontine. As sort of promise. An investment shared between friends. A commitment which grows even when one party dies. A tontine is a promise shared by survivors."

"But if there was only the two of you, then haven't you become the only survivor?" I asked.

Sterling looked at the two Decks. "No. We have become the survivors. I know you think that Don died the year after he left the Academy, but I'd like to think that he's still here."

I smiled. "He is. I'm sure of that."

"Then, Don, take note. I'm about to keep our promise." Sterling held up his double-sealed card. "You got one in your Deck. Find it."

I always wanted to know the secret held within the confines of that card and now it was about to be released. Not by me though ... by a friend.

Like a child holding out his last candy, I placed my secret card on top of my new Deck.

"We glued them around the edges, but I'm sure you've discovered already there is one corner left unsealed."

Slowly I inspected the card and located the corner.

"Don and I each wrote a special message on our sealed card then exchanged them. We hoped we would meet again some day and open them together. The deal was simple. On these two cards we each wrote the most valuable lesson the other had taught us. This one lesson was to be held above all others."

Schlitz's eyes filled with the tears of a long lost memory. "If one of us died before we could meet again, we promised each other we would find a new friend with which we could share...."

"Sarge, I...."

"Sshhh."

In one move he pulled his card apart and laid it on the table. I did the same with mine.

The messages were identical:

In order to find a friend —
you must first be one.

We read the cards. Together. Silently.

Sterling's eyes met mine and I knew I had found a new friend. Don Withers had taught me well. I knew that I would always love, cherish and honor him as a friend, but it was Schlitz who had ridden with me, safely tucked away in my briefcase. It was Schlitz who spoke to me from a worn Deck of cards, in my darkest hours. Schlitz!

That was the day I remember most. Even after his death, Don was able to reach out and teach. He taught me friendship and a new life. Both were necessary if I was to continue His work.

A handshake, a few tears and an embrace shared between friends. Sterling was no longer my enemy.

"The responsibility doesn't end here, you know." Sterling spoke clearly as he rubbed his shoulder.

"I understand," I replied. "When we leave here this morning, we leave with a promise to pass on our learning."

"To each person we meet." Schlitz looked down at his Deck. "There goes my fishbowl — I guess I'll even have to start feeding Smokey."

"He likes cheese," I suggested.

"I know. So do I." Schlitz managed the biggest laugh I had ever heard.

We looked at each other. Two very old Friends had just met. Shared. Laughed.

One hour later, Sterling and I parted company. We both went home. Changed.

Don had led the way for both of us and a promise was made to pass on the Decks, their wisdom — and our Friendship.

Thanks, Don.

Each star represents five years of service.

CHAPTER TEN

CLOUDS

The day most wasted,
is the one —
You never want back.

I walked out of the police station, past a parade of freshly released, wandering drunks, and across the parking lot to my car. In my left hand was my canvas duty bag, and in my right I carried my old tattered leather briefcase. Neither seemed as heavy as they did at the beginning of the night shift.

As I breathed in the fresh morning air, the journey across the parking lot seemed short. I felt light. I stood by my car for a moment and smiled at the drunks looking for the nearest bus stop. I suppose we all had a destination, even the lost ones who didn't know where they were going.

Reaching down, I slid the keys into the car door lock and turned. The lock did not stick as it usually did and, as I pulled the door open, it refused to groan and squeak like most 10-year-old cars. I threw my duty bag in the back seat and my briefcase on the front passenger's seat.

Taking my place behind the wheel, I slammed the door. A new presence made itself known. A Deck. A new Deck. It pushed against my chest as a reminder of the morning.

"Well, let's see how they work." I mouthed the words and laid the tattered handkerchief on the seat beside me.

Shuffle. Cut. Turn over a new card:

The noblest of all places on earth is where an ancient hatred has become — a present forgiveness!

I looked out through my windshield into a new morning. A very noble morning. The sun rose brightly over a new world. Birds sang and the big white fluffy clouds that floated by held a thousand images for a child to see.

Except for one cloud!

Alone, amongst the others, it reflected the morning light — clear, clean and simple — and if I held my head just right it looked down on me like the face of

An Old Friend.

APPENDIX: THE DECK

It was a cold winter night in 1968 when Corporal Don Withers gave me his copy of "The Deck". Since that night, his wisdom and the subsequent messages derived from Sergeant Sterling Schilitz's deck have guided me through thirty years of service in the RCMP. I have consulted The Deck while enjoying my greatest successes and coping with my greatest failures and during both the happiest and saddest times of my life. Always, the documented wisdom of these two friends has served as a guiding light, emotionally, morally, and spiritually.

After Don Withers gave me his Deck and I came more and more to appreciate its content, I vowed that I would share his words with future friends as they passed through my life. As he had suggested, I have added to his thoughts some of the personal insights and revelations that three decades have given me. (I think it was his way of saying The Deck should never be cast in stone.)

During my career The Deck has been a living, ever-changing thing as I have added my own thoughts and occasionally modified others. What follows is my current Deck for all who have taken the time to read our story.

This is now your Deck to embrace and incorporate into daily life. With it comes a responsibility of sharing and promoting its wisdom. I encourage you to add your own experience and refinements—and—with kindness, once again pass it on to a friend.

You are welcome to make copies of the enclosed for your personal use. I offer this deck to you in memory of my good friend, Corporal Don Withers.

Robert G. (Bob) Teather
October, 1997

This section has been designed to allow the owner of this book to copy and clip The Deck for their personal use.

Two blank cards below may be used to create personal additions to The Deck

In Memory of: *Cpl. Don Withers*

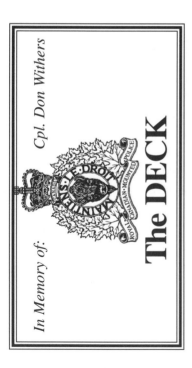

The DECK

We must give up what we are - in order to discover what we might become.

In order to be human - you must first do a humanitarian act.

Good-byes are a necessary pause - before good friends can meet again.

The best mirror is found in the eyes of a friend.

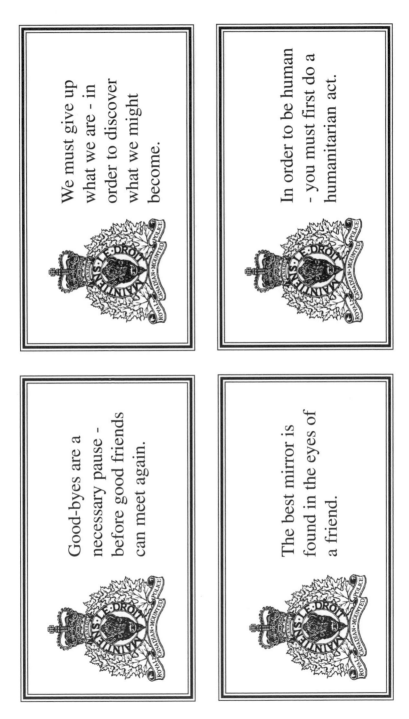

115

Ignorance has two
traps:
Believing what isn't
so and
Not believing what
is.

We should never
learn to forget:

Even a fool when
quiet, appears wise.

Nothing is so strong
as true gentleness:
Or
As gentle as true
strength.

The injuries we inflict and the injuries that we see are always measured on different scales.

Tell me - I forget.
Show me - I remember.
Involve me - I understand.

The best way to get out of difficulty is to go through it.

Worry is the darkroom, where negative thoughts are developed.

You cannot do a kindness too soon, because — you never know how soon it will be too late.

It is easier to fight for your principles than to live up to them.

Teach a child not to step on a frog. It's good for the child and better for the frog.

Imagine your world, perfect in every way. Then be humbled, for God has already imagined it - much better!

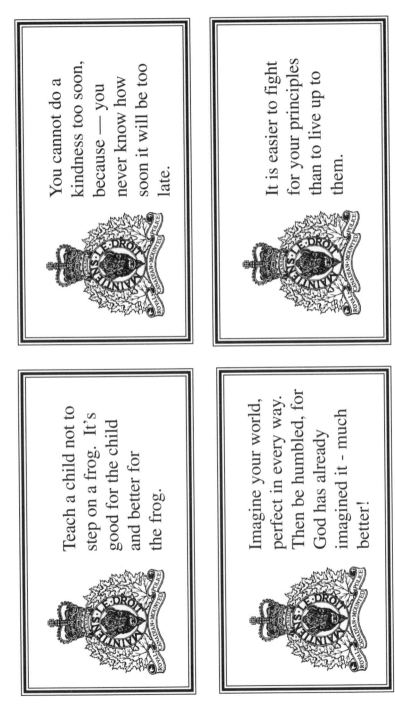

Would the child you were, be proud of the adult you have become?

The man who judges doesn't matter - Because the man who matters, never judges.

Every day is created perfect. The imperfection lies only in what we do with it.

The noblest of all places on Earth, is where an ancient hatred has become a present forgiveness.

The saddest words of God and men - are in the phrase,

"It might have been."

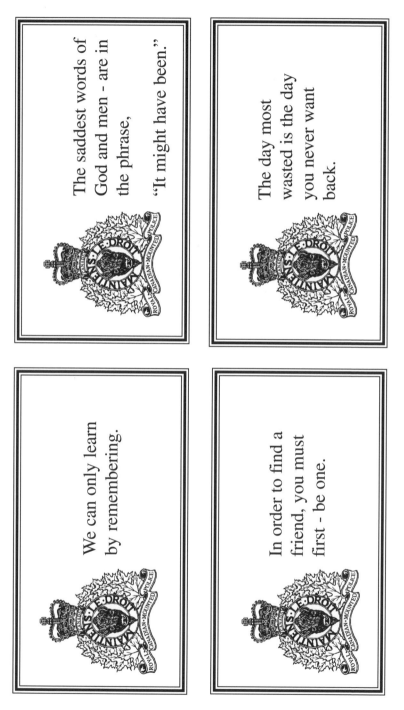

The day most wasted is the day you never want back.

We can only learn by remembering.

In order to find a friend, you must first - be one.

Born out of sharing, miracles are natural. When miracles stop occurring - something has gone wrong.

Anything we do may be unimportant.

But it is important that we do it anyway.

"Impossible" only defines the degree of difficulty.

It's not whether you win or lose -

It's how you hold the trophy.

The only thing necessary for the triumph of evil is for good people to do nothing.

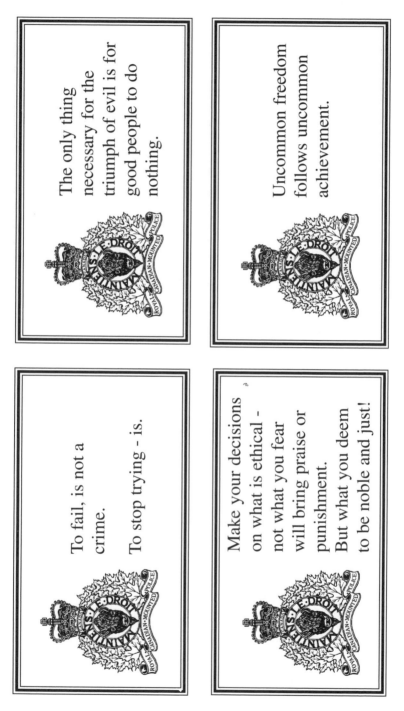

Uncommon freedom follows uncommon achievement.

To fail, is not a crime.

To stop trying - is.

Make your decisions on what is ethical - not what you fear will bring praise or punishment.
But what you deem to be noble and just!

They hurt or heal,
Create pain or
growth.
They are - your
words.

Future generations will
not judge us on how we
treated ourselves or
each other. Future
generations will judge
us on how we treated
our animals.

The kindest deed
you can do, is to
help another person
and not get caught.

To know who you
are and where you
are going - is but the
first step of your
journey.

Behind us - only
memories.

Ahead of us - only
dreams.

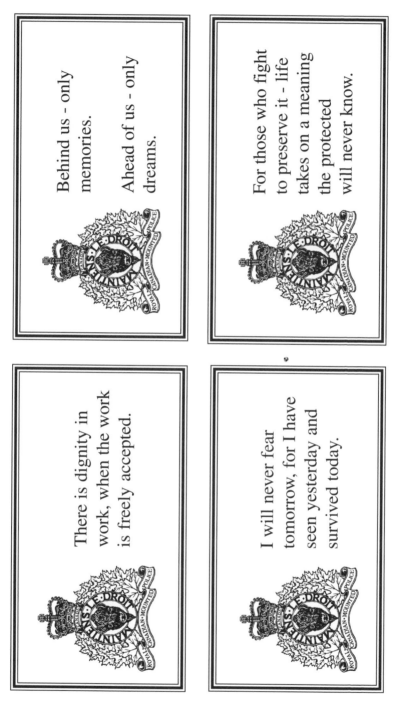

For those who fight
to preserve it - life
takes on a meaning
the protected
will never know.

There is dignity in
work, when the work
is freely accepted.

I will never fear
tomorrow, for I have
seen yesterday and
survived today.

Failure is not an option!

Faithless is he that says farewell - when the road darkens.

The game ain't over yet.

Your will and courage to overcome obstacles are more important than the events that occur around you.

True freedom and strength are found only within the confines of unwavering discipline.

To be a winner, all you need to give- is- everything you have.

There is no such thing as false hope.

All hope is true.

Limitations are those spiteful little hindrances we set upon ourselves.

Never surrender your principles.

Without them, you are nothing.

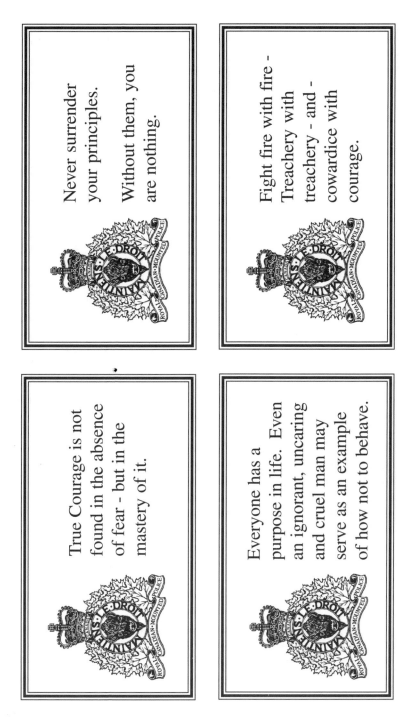

Fight fire with fire - Treachery with treachery - and - cowardice with courage.

True Courage is not found in the absence of fear - but in the mastery of it.

Everyone has a purpose in life. Even an ignorant, uncaring and cruel man may serve as an example of how not to behave.

OTHER BOOKS
BY ROBERT GORDON TEATHER

Scarlet Tunic Vol.2
Robert Gordon Teather

*We are strong at times but weak at others.
Often we revel . . . yet just as often we choke
back tears—horribly sad tears—that we are
taught never to reveal.*

This popular sequel exposes a blend of heart
rendering admission and late night hi-jinx among
the men and women officers that make up a
suburban Mountie detachment.

*"Many of us feel the time has come to reveal the
mystery behind the Scarlet Tunic."*

ISBN 1-895811-01-5
5 1/2" x 8 1/2" • 128 pages
Softcover • $11.95

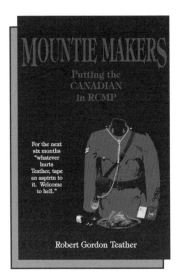

Mountie Makers
Robert Gordon Teather

Corporal Teather's story brings you close to six
young men from across Canada. These
characters capture the essence of Canada and
demonstrate an enlightening aspect of the
RCMP recruitment and training process. After a
29-year, active career Bob has come to realize
that it is Basic Training that puts the Canadian
in RCMP and bonds its members into a force
capable of policing our complex country.

ISBN 1-895811-41-4
5 1/2" x 8 1/2" • 160 pages
Softcover • $14.95